Julien,
I hope you enjoy
my story.
Life can be tough
but I learned to
Never Tap Out!
Ed

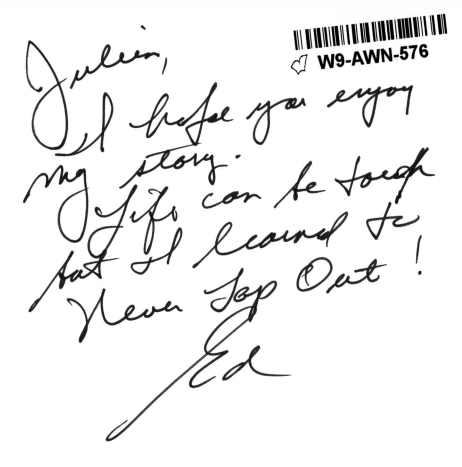

To Julien,
Hope you enjoy!
- Kevin Cowhes

WAY DOWN IN THE HOLE

The Meteoric Rise, Tragic Fall
and Ultimate Redemption
of America's Most Promising Cop

WAY DOWN IN THE HOLE

The Meteoric Rise, Tragic Fall and Ultimate Redemption of America's Most Promising Cop

Ed Norris
with Kevin Cowherd

Apprentice House
Loyola University Maryland
Baltimore, Maryland

This book is a work of fiction and any coincidence with real life people is purely the imagination of the author.

First Edition

Printed in the United States of America

Hardcover ISBN: 978-1-62720-144-5
Paperback ISBN: 978-1-62720-145-2
E-book ISBN: 978-1-62720-146-9

Design: Apprentice House

Published by Apprentice House

Apprentice House
Loyola University Maryland
4501 N. Charles Street
Baltimore, MD 21210
410.617.5265 • 410.617.2198 (fax)
www.ApprenticeHouse.com
info@ApprenticeHouse.com

When you walk through the garden
You gotta watch your back
Well, I beg your pardon
Walk the straight and narrow track
If you walk with Jesus
He's gonna save your soul
You gotta keep the devil down in the hole.

— *Tom Waits, Way Down in the Hole*

I dedicate this book to my son Jack, whose love and mere presence in my life gave me the strength to endure it all. And to my ex-wife Kathryn, who was my rock during this witch hunt. She remains in my heart and will forever be my "ride or die chick."

FOREWORD

David Simon

Sixteen years into the rearview:

I am sitting in an Italian restaurant on Baltimore's Charles Street, picking at a salad, trying to make nice with the city's new police commissioner, a thick, fire-hydrant of a guy with a rampant New York accent. He's telling cop stories. Talking cop shit. I've traded in the stuff for years, first as a reporter and now as a television writer, and the patter of the new boss is no better or worse than many.

A case here, an anecdote there; I pair a crouton with an anchovy and lift my fork toward my face, giving a slight nod as if I actually give a damn. Because, to be honest, this lunch was scheduled as simply a polite curtain-raiser, a friendly shot-across-the-bow to let the man know that we would soon be filming another television drama in Baltimore. This one would be darker than the last. This one would critique the drug war harshly.

"Feel free," he says, when I finally get around to my purpose. "The drug war is so fucked up."

I note this with much surprise: More honesty from a Baltimore police commander than I am accustomed. On the other hand, this lunch is off the record.

"Well, I just thought it fair to let you know what will be coming if HBO picks the show up," I reiterate. "It will not be a comfortable depiction of a police department lost in drug prohibition."

He bolts his drink, shrugs: "You do what you do. And I'll do what I do."

Mission accomplished. We settle back into a reverie of cop humor, stationhouse tales and good, solid casework.

"I always liked Baltimore. I first came here on a case like, 10, 12 years ago. Great fucking case . . ."

Ah Christ. Here we go again. Some long tale of some ancient moment when this guy got to hear the handcuffs click and all was right with the world. I pretend to listen, but really, I confess that my mind is wandering. He rambles through the details of a New York murder by a Baltimore drug trafficker, a tip that the gun was down here in Maryland, the lure of the dealer to an interrogation in Manhattan and the simultaneous rush south to get a search warrant and find the weapon. I'm thinking about the desert menu. Until:

"So we hit the house with the Baltimore guys and what I remember is that every drawer we open, under the mattress, every goddamn closet, there's just all this porn. And not just regular porn, but fat girl porn. I mean really big ladies. This guy was really into big women . . ."

He laughs, remembering.

"Anyway, we found this gun in an upstairs closet."

I damn near drop my fork.

"Maurice Proctor."

He looks at me strangely.

"Maurice Proctor was your shooter. Nine hundred block of Northern Parkway. You hit the house with Roger Nolan's squad . . ."

"How did you . . .?"

"And, motherfucker, you didn't find the gun. I did. Third floor, back bedroom. In a green duffel. Under a bunch of fat girl magazines. Me and Donald Kincaid."

And so ends the anecdote of the second time I met Eddie Norris, 12 years after I watched him put down a 1988 murder – a minor footnote in a year I spent in the Baltimore homicide unit to write a book – and perhaps another eighteen months before the broadcast of

"The Wire" on HBO.

By the end of that lunch, I came to realize that whatever else the powers that be had managed to do in Baltimore, they had, for once, chosen a working cop to command its long-suffering, increasingly over-whelmed police department.

It might seem that knowing how to do police work would be an elemental skill set for anyone asked to command a major police department. It is not. There are two hierarchies in any such agency: one is the hierarchy of rank, and the other of policing, the acquired and honed ability to lock the right asshole up when a city most needs it, when the crime really matters. Seldom does anyone rising on one totem show any talent for the other.

Norris was one of the few exceptions in my memory. And for a brief period in Baltimore's modern history, he turned the slow, lumbering old freighter that is the Baltimore Police Department hard to starboard and got some people to do police work. That is neither as simple or as permanent an accomplishment as it sounds, and after accomplishing much in the first year or two, the usual political venalities and easy rhetoric began their inevitable attrition. He also made enemies. But then a good man it is routinely said, is known by his enemies.

In the end, the battle would see him walking not only from the Baltimore department, but from law enforcement, which, grievously, is his life's calling. If you know the tale – and I'm sure you will, if you have picked up this memoir – his banishment and the tarring of his reputation have more to do with fundamental questions about institutional law enforcement and political maneuver than the rote assertions of corruption. Suffice to say that an old stationhouse proverb is true in all respects: If the sonsabitches want you, they got you.

As a lark, when he was still police commissioner, we cast Eddie Norris as a working cop, a homicide detective who knew his business. That was, to us, an inside joke. But more than that, it was my nod to the fact that singularly among most of the command staff in so many departmental regimes, this man actually knew why good police work matters. And why bad police work matters, too. And when Norris was struggling, we made sure to keep his character in our fictional world. He was made to give up so much; knowing the whole story, we could not ask him to give up more.

Here's the whole of his tale.

David Simon
Baltimore, Md.
November 27, 2016

INTRODUCTION
Keeping the Rats Out

People always ask me what the worst moment was. That one's easy. The worst moment was like something from a Fellini movie.

The time: September of 2004. The place: the U.S. Federal Penitentiary, Atlanta, a shadowy Gothic-looking structure with gun turrets looming over high stone walls that emitted a strange greenish glow.

Months earlier, I had stood in front of a Baltimore courtroom packed with family, friends and national media and listened in stunned disbelief as a judge sentenced me to six months in prison on trumped-up charges of corruption and tax evasion.

Now, after serving time in Florida and Mississippi, I'd been transferred to Atlanta, one of the most notorious lock-ups in the country.

It was my first night in the "Big House" and the guards had just escorted me through a corridor ringed by howling inmates to a sweltering cell. My two new cellies were straight out of Central Casting: hulking, sullen and inked from head to toe with garish testimonials to the thug life. Neither seemed thrilled to be sharing his quarters with another wretched guest of the government.

Gazing around, I noticed there were only two bunks. Guess who was sleeping on the floor? I sighed and threw down my newly-issued pillow and blanket.

As I spread out on the hard concrete, one of my cheerful new roomies handed me a tube of rolled-up newspapers wrapped in tape. He pointed at the cell's battleship-gray steel door.

"Hold that roll under the door with your feet," he said. "It'll keep the rats out."

Rats?!

Really?!

With that, he turned around and fired up a meth pipe. Soon he and his charming companion were beaming upward into another world, the dope leaving them giggling and muttering gibberish to each other.

Watching this surreal scene, I began to laugh uncontrollably.

It was the shrill, frenzied laughter of someone on the edge of a crack-up.

Look at me! I thought. *I'm wearing orange prison pants that are way too small and a T-shirt the size of a Bedouin's tent. They didn't even give me sneakers that match! Meanwhile, my welcoming committee over there is getting blasted on meth and I'm crumpled on the floor like some kind of skid row Orkin Man, trying to keep the rats out!*

A year ago, I was the superintendent of the Maryland State Police! Before that I was the police commissioner of Baltimore! How the fuck did they ever get away with this?!

I stifled a sob. Sleep didn't come for hours as the absurdity of my situation plunged me deeper and deeper into despair.

Prison?!?

Me?

In the same place where they locked up Al Capone?

The same place the Cuban "Mariel boatlift" detainees burned in the late 80's riots?

How could any of this be real?!

All my life, I'd thought of myself as one of the good guys. You could say I was born to be a cop. My father had been a cop. So had my grandfather. So had four uncles.

As a boy growing up in Brooklyn, N.Y., I thought of the police as super-heroes. Instead of colorful capes and tights and masks, they wore crisp uniform shirts with brass buttons and blue woolen jackets, shiny badges on their chests and no-nonsense Smith & Wesson revolvers on their hips. They were fearless and taciturn and had each other's backs no matter what. Everyone in the neighborhood looked up to them.

Little wonder that at age 20, I went into the family business and joined the New York Police Department, determined to do my part in the endless war against the bad guys. There was certainly no shortage of them. Mid-town Manhattan, my first assignment, was a toxic stew of stick-up boys, drug dealers, pimps, hookers, pickpockets, car thieves and con men preying on the wide-eyed tourists and down-and-out drifters that poured off the buses daily at the Port Authority.

For a rookie cop who craved action, who relished breaking up a good old-fashioned poolroom brawl or rolling around the sidewalk with a twitchy junkie flashing a knife, it was intoxicating.

Once, working plain-clothes on 42nd Street, I saw this guy smack a girl across the face. I was wearing a red-white-and-blue satin USA jacket, the gold Olympic rings gleaming in the late-day sunshine.

The guy saw me staring at him and smirked.

"What are *you* going to do about it, Captain America?" he said. "You want to be a hero?"

Yep, I sure did.

I hit this fool so hard that when my partner Dan Mullin joined the fracas, the three of us went crashing through the doors of a Popeye's before I could get out the handcuffs.

Captain America?

Hell, I was starting to feel like him!

From the beginning, I was on the fast track in the NYPD, shooting up the ranks in anti-crime, narcotics, the detective bureau. I headed the warrant division and we doubled the yearly number of fugitives caught from 6,000 to 12,000. I was put in charge of the department's first Cold Case Squad, which won national acclaim and was the subject of a best-selling book and NPR special.

In the eyes of the brass, I was now a genuine superstar. And at the tender age of 36, I was named deputy commissioner of operations, the youngest in the department's history.

My star kept rising. When I took over as commissioner of the Baltimore Police Department in 2000, the city's murder rate was seven times the national average. Over 300 homicides had been recorded each year for the past decade.

Morale in the department was horrible. Corruption was pervasive. Modern policing equipment was largely non-existent.

But with the eager blessing of the city's charismatic new mayor, Martin O'Malley – the newspaper called us "Batman and Robin" – I set out to change all that. And we did. Crime went down almost immediately, dropping 29 percent the first two years. The murder rate plummeted from 305 to 262 the first year, to 253 the year after that.

And when I jumped out of a police car at a busy drug corner to wrestle a heroin dealer to the ground – "Unit One in pursuit!" squawked over the radio – it only heightened the mythology already building around me.

The new commish did what?

Ran down a corner boy and put the cuffs on him?

No one had ever heard of such a thing.

It was clear that crime in Baltimore was undergoing a seismic shift for the better. The bad guys were on the run. The streets felt safer. I was a rock star. I ate in the city's best restaurants and drank in the finest bars. Men elbowed each other aside to buy me another round. Women wanted to be near me.

I had a recurring role on "The Wire," HBO's hit police drama, playing a street detective from New York named – wait for it – Ed Norris. Even when I became burned out and disillusioned and took the top job with the Maryland State Police in 2002, I remained hugely popular in Baltimore.

Veteran cops, city council members and ordinary citizens would say I was the best police commissioner the city had ever had.

The business school at the University of Virginia would teach a graduate class about how my leadership skills transformed the police department.

I felt bigger than Cal Ripken Jr.

Then it all came crashing down.

It started with stories in the *Baltimore Sun* about an off-the-books expense account while I was still the city's police commissioner. This was followed by the steady drip-drip-drip of ominous rumors about an investigation by the U.S. Attorney's office.

At first I was unconcerned. The account involved no taxpayer money. Zero.

But the feds wanted their pound of flesh. Their claws were in me. And they had no intention of letting go.

Even after an independent audit showed almost all the money was spent on departmental business, even after I paid back $20,000 in personal expenses for which the receipts had been lost, federal prosecutors brought a sham indictment that included lurid allegations of gifts spent on women at Victoria's Secret and extra-marital affairs.

Now the case contained the whiff of sex.

And we all know what that can do in today's over-heated media climate.

The feds went into over-drive looking for dirt on my love life. The press beat me like a piñata. It was all so sickeningly unfair. And I had to sit back and take it.

Let me say this up front: I was a damned good police commissioner in those days. But I was no angel. I strayed in my marriage. I worked hard and partied hard. And some of that partying was with women I had no business being with.

But this is the truth: I never stole even one thin dime from that fund. Never used it to pay for gifts for anyone except my staff, such as flowers for my secretaries and holsters for my bodyguards. Bottom line? I never abused that fund in any way, shape or form.

Of course, I pleaded not guilty to the charges.

"It's all bullshit," I told my lawyers. "Let's go to trial."

I wanted to take on the bastards.

But you go up against the federal government at your peril. Those guys don't like to lose. They have armies of lawyers and an endless supply of cash to throw at you.

So it was that a few months later, I lay in a dank cell in the Atlanta penitentiary, half-crazed with fear and anxiety, listening to the giddy ravings of a couple of dopers as I pressed my shaking feet against the bars and prayed for the rodent hordes to stay away.

So this is my story.

It's the story of a good cop's life, his exemplary 23-year career and the dark forces that eventually took him down.

It's a cautionary tale about government over-reach and naked prosecutorial ambition that can seemingly target any public figure at any time for any reason.

And maybe my story can also serve as a primer of sorts for how to rebuild a life after you're stamped with the permanent tag of "convicted felon," a situation familiar to far too many men and women in this country.

In the words of the great Tom Waits, I was way down in the hole. So far down you could have whacked me over the head with a shovel and buried me with a few more scoops of dirt.

This is the story of how I got so low.

And the story of how I dug myself out.

1

From Brooklyn to the
Land of Lacoste

My father, Ed Norris, became a New York City policeman when he was 33 years old and I was seven. Before that he had been a butcher. Even then I knew how dangerous a cop's life could be. Cutting and packaging meat in a cozy store seemed far safer and less stressful than patrolling the treacherous streets of the Big Apple, where more than a few of the citizens tended to greet the presence of a blue uniform by reaching for a weapon.

"Why would you leave the other job?" I remember asking my dad. "Why would you do *this*?"

"Somebody has to," he replied.

It sounds like a line from an old Western, something the square-jawed hero says as he hoists his shotgun and goes off to face the gang of gimlet-eyed gunslingers terrorizing the sleepy cattle town. But those words stuck with me forever.

It didn't help my anxiety levels – or those of my mother, Catherine, and my special-needs younger brother, Robert – that my father worked in the 77th Precinct in Brooklyn's Bedford-Stuyvesant neighborhood, one of the most dangerous parts of the city. And it *sure* didn't help when, after he'd been on the job just four years, the Black Liberation Army began assassinating police officers.

The BLA was a radical, underground organization in the early 1970's that had vowed to take up arms "for the liberation and self-determination of black people in the U.S." In time, it would be blamed for the murders of some 13 police officers, including the high-profile New York ambush slayings of Officers Joseph Piagentini and Waverly Jones in May of 1971, and the executions of officers Rocco Laurie and Gregory Foster in January of 1972.

From the beginning, it was clear that the cops were severely outgunned by the BLA. The BLA's murderous followers were armed with rifles and machine guns while the police carried .38 specials, six-shot revolvers that were no match for heavier firepower.

To even the odds, off-duty officers began backing up on-duty cops. I remember my father's friends coming over to our house in Flatlands with their hunting rifles and shotguns, whatever they had, and loading them with ammunition. I remember my father emptying a box of bullets and filling his pockets with them.

Then these off-duty cops, dressed in street clothes and driving their personal cars, would go back to the 77th precinct. There they'd monitor their precinct radios and shadow the on-duty cops when they responded to even the most innocuous calls: disorderly male, suspicious package – anything that could lure an unsuspecting officer into a BLA ambush.

I remember being terrified of what could happen to my father and his friends. But I was proud of them, too.

This is pretty cool, that these guys would do this for each other, I remember thinking. And seeing this "Brotherhood of Blue" come to life in my living room every night stirred in me the first inklings that someday maybe I could be a cop, too.

I learned early in life that my father was never truly off-duty, either. He was a hard-working guy who had grown up extremely poor. His mother raised six children by herself after his father died – from alcoholism, we think. What we *know* is that the family would get evicted from their apartments all the time for non-payment of rent

– my dad talked often about sitting on the curb with the furniture as a kid after another hard-hearted landlord had tossed them out.

Maybe that explains why my dad couldn't stand idly by and watch people be mistreated – whether he was in uniform or not.

One day when I was 12 – just after we had moved to Flatlands, a neighborhood near the south shore of Brooklyn – he was driving me home from a doctor's appointment when we heard a woman's cries for help.

My father threw the car in park. Without a word, he leaped out and began running in the direction of the screams. It turned out a woman had just been mugged. A couple of moments later, he returned, huffing and puffing, and gave the grateful woman back her purse.

I had been frightened when my father took off after the bad guys. He was all by himself, after all, and this was long before the era of cell phones. When he finally came back to the car and filled me in on what happened, I didn't feel much better.

The foot chase had been brief – he had run down the muggers, two teenagers, and drawn his gun on them.

Suddenly, one had whirled and thrown the woman's purse at him. Then the two muggers had vaulted a fence and escaped.

At a time when police officers were being killed at a rate of about 10 per year, my father's actions struck me as incredibly brave, but incredibly risky, too. But as I was to learn over and over again, there was little about being a cop that didn't involve risk.

By the time I was in high school, I was learning first-hand about how dangerous the streets could be – and not just for the police. Brooklyn Tech was one of the top schools in the city, specializing in science, math and engineering. But it was in Fort Greene, a rough neighborhood, and the white kids who attended it were often the targets for muggings, assaults and robberies.

On my first day of school there, an older guy walked up to me with a bunch of his friends. Just like that – *BAM!* – he hauled off and slapped me in the face. It began a long pattern of intimidation that many of my friends and I would be subjected to for the next four years. It also solidified my life-long hatred of bullies.

One day I was so tired of being victimized that I took the subway all the way to Sheepshead Bay, the last stop for the D train. It was a fisherman's haven in those days, with a number of fishing supply stores scattered about.

I bought a big knife and carried it every single day for the rest of my high school career. I never stabbed anyone. But I pulled it out a couple times to let guys know I wasn't fucking around when they started their usual menacing bullshit.

I joined the football team my sophomore year. We didn't have a home field, so we practiced on a crappy city park field some distance away, underneath the Brooklyn-Queens Expressway.

To get there, we had to walk through Fort Greene Park and the nearby housing projects, where they would routinely welcome us with bottles, bricks and rocks tossed from the roofs of the buildings. We weren't the brightest kids around, but we soon figured out it was a good idea to leave our helmets on during these walks.

We even had a sniper use us for target practice one afternoon in the projects. He was on one of the roofs, firing at us with a rifle. He didn't hit anyone and the police soon arrested him, which was a cause for celebration. But even when we started two-a-days, the harassment never stopped. After we'd change into our uniforms on the field and leave our clothes on the sidelines, the neighborhood kids would go through our pockets and steal our money while we were doing drills or scrimmaging.

Every once in a while, though, there would be small moral victories that would buoy our sense of justice and fair play.

One day, a couple of my teammates were walking ahead of the rest of us on our way home from practice. As the two rounded the corner, they were set upon by a pair of older guys who tried to rob them.

When the rest of us came upon the scene, we quickly unstrapped our helmets from our military duffle bags and proceeded to beat the crap out of the two muggers. Someone called the police and a few transit cops ran up from the nearby subway station.

This would prove to be my very first take on the powers of police discretion. Because by the time the cops got there, the bad guys were bloodied and bruised and splayed out on the sidewalk. The cops could have probably busted us for assault. But they knew the two local scumbags who had tried to rob us and quickly sized up what had happened.

"Get out of here," one cop said with a wave of his hand.

How about that? Common sense had prevailed! The police realized there was no point locking up a bunch of kids who had essentially been crime victims a few minutes earlier.

Maybe all of this made us tougher than a lot of other football teams. In any event, we were good – very good. We were 6-2-1 my senior year and lost in the playoffs to Bayside High, which ended up winning the city championship.

At least four of my teammates went on to play at Division I schools, and a bunch of others got scholarships and aid to go to D-II and D-III schools, too. As for me, an undersized outside linebacker with more heart than talent, I would go off to D-III University of Rochester, where I'd be converted into a safety.

Rochester, on the southern shore of Lake Ontario in western New York State, was booming when I arrived on campus in the summer of 1978. Multi-national corporations such as Kodak, Xerox and Bausch & Lomb were going great guns and pouring gobs of money into the school.

The university was considered a "rich kids" haven, filled with moneyed undergrads who couldn't get into Harvard, Yale, Williams, etc. I was there because it was a great science school and I had aced my physics exams. I had also actually begun to dream about becoming a doctor.

But for a poor kid from Brooklyn just getting by on a package of loans, scholarships, federal grants and on-campus work opportunities, the U of Rochester was a total cultural shock.

Let's start with how I looked back then.

Remember, this was the summer of '78. What was in the movies? Right, the monster blockbuster "Saturday Night Fever." And like a lot of other Brooklyn kids, I fancied myself another Tony Manero, the John Travolta character who worked in a paint store and lived for the weekends so he and his buddies could dance all night in glittering discos.

Blow-back haircut, paisley shirts, leather jackets, white suits – oh, yeah, that was me. And now I was going to this fancy-ass school with all these preppy kids who were definitely *not* dressed like me. It was the first time I'd ever seen L.L. Bean duck boots. Not to mention pink Lacoste shirts worn with the collars popped.

It was the kind of place where kids were going to Aspen and Switzerland over Christmas break.

When I came back to school after my first year, a girl asked me: "So . . . where did you summer?"

Where did I what?

Summer?

I had no idea what she was talking about. I'd never heard the term before.

"Well," she said, "I went to Italy."

Ohhhh, I said. Well, I sold shoes at a mall in Brooklyn.

That's how I *summered.*

But even if I didn't totally assimilate at Rochester, I thrived. I loved college. I was promptly recruited by the two jock fraternities and joined Theta Delta Chi. This was a football/lacrosse fraternity, and I quickly found myself surrounded by smart, ultra-competitive people.

The football was great, too. The team went 5-4 my first year. As a freshman, I didn't start, but traveled to away games as part of the kickoff team. No one on the roster, least of all me, was under any delusions that we were headed for the NFL. And if I ever did entertain such a notion, events on the field would quickly bring me back down to earth.

Once, when we were playing the University of Buffalo on a freezing, rainy day at ancient War Memorial Stadium, the former home of the Buffalo Bills, the coaches put me in to defend on a two-point conversion try. UB had a receiver who was also a world-class sprinter, so everyone knew they would throw the ball.

Sure enough, UB threw the ball. And my jersey was practically on fire when Mr. World-Class Speed blew past me for the score with whatever remnants of the tiny, chilled crowd still remained. But football kept me in shape. And it was the perfect sport for a kid who liked to hit – sometimes a bit too much.

That off-season, one of my on-campus jobs was as a security guard. Many of the football players had similar jobs – we'd accompany armed security guards on patrol. One night, as this older security guard and I made our rounds, we saw a kid breaking into a car.

The kid spotted us and took off.

"I'll get him," I said.

The older security guard rolled his eyes.

"Yeah, sure," he said sarcastically. "You'll get him."

But why *wouldn't* I get him? I was a defensive back on the football team. I was also pretty fast for a white guy. And I was in great shape.

Anyway, I ran this would-be thief down easily and tackled him. We were rolling around on the sidewalk when it looked to me like he was going for something in his waistband.

A knife? A gun?

I didn't know for sure. And I wasn't about to ask.

So I hit him – *WHAM!* – with a left hook. The guy went limp. Seconds later, his eyes just blew up. From the swelling, I knew he was hurt.

The kid was locked up, but that wasn't the end of the story – at least not for me.

Instead, I was brought up on charges by the student-faculty disciplinary council, who thought I had used excessive force during the incident. Now they were threatening to kick me out of school.

At a hearing in front of the council a couple of weeks later, the guy I had hit was brought in as a witness. He still had blood in his eye, which wasn't exactly helpful for my defense. I repeated the story of what had happened from the time we saw the kid breaking into the car.

"But why did you *hit* him?" a council member demanded.

"I thought he was going for a weapon," I said. "I saw him reaching for his waistband."

Now they all seemed incredulous.

"Why would you think he's going for a *weapon*?" they asked.

"Well," I said, "where I come from, *everyone* carries a weapon. At least a knife."

Now they seemed even more incredulous.

"Where did you grow up?" they asked.

"Brooklyn," I said.

"*Ohhhh,*" they all said in unison, nodding as if a great revelation had suddenly dawned on them.

In the end, they decided not to kick the poor kid from Brooklyn out of school. Instead, they just rewrote the security training guide, probably something to the effect: Try not to batter the local car thieves and cause retinal damage if humanly possible.

But by that summer, it was clear that the kid from Brooklyn was literally too damn poor to continue attending ritzy U of Rochester.

My parents couldn't afford to help me with tuition or room and board, and my aid package was falling short. But I desperately wanted to return to school. So I decided to work as an exterminator, save my money and go back to Rochester at some point.

That winter, on a whim, I took the train up to school and visited my frat buddies. I had so much fun I decided to stick around for a while, which didn't exactly sit well with my parents.

Then, at the school's Winter Carnival, I got into a brawl with this big, drunk townie who was hassling my buddy's girlfriend.

After the townie and I exchanged a few pleasantries – it ended with him calling me a "fucking stupid football player" – I popped him hard enough that they had to call an ambulance. My friends all grabbed me and told me to run before the cops came, since I'd already been in trouble at the school.

When the assistant football coach, John Vitone, got wind of all this, he sat me down and said: "You want to fight? OK, you can fight." It turned out his friend, the sheriff of Monroe County, had a boxing club. I had boxed in Police Athletic League centers in New York when I was 16 and 17, and I took to it again with renewed interest – if only to stay out of trouble.

Suddenly, it seemed as though things were looking up again.

Coach Vitone, who was a mentor to me, helped me get a little more money from the school. I stayed there for the spring semester, rejoined the football team and came back in the summer for two-a-day workouts to start the new season.

Which is when everything blew up in my face again.

One day before practice, I was summoned to the dean's office. The conversation started on a promising note as he read from my transcript.

"You're a dean's list student, a varsity athlete and a fraternity member," he began. "You're such an asset to this campus."

Listening to this, I puffed out my chest.

Damn right! I thought, as if a cartoon bubble had suddenly appeared over my head. *This is gonna be great! I see a bagful of money coming! More financial aid! Maybe some kind of big grant or scholarship add-on!*

Instead, it turned out to be, uh, exactly none of those things.

"You know," the dean went on, "you should really look into a state university. Because I don't see how you're going to make this work financially."

I was stunned as I left his office. In possibly the most low-key and polite way ever, I had just been thrown out of college.

Great, I thought. *How's that for hitting the trifecta? No college. No job. And my parents are rip-shit pissed at me. Going home should be loads of fun.*

Arriving back in Brooklyn in late August, I was notified that the New York Police Department was installing a new class of recruits. At the urging of my father, I had taken the written exam – and aced it – back in high school. My dad had always considered a police job to be a great back-up plan for me.

But when the last class of recruits had been installed, I was only 19 and the hiring age was 20. Now, though, there was nothing preventing me from going into the police academy and beginning my new career.

Except . . . I wasn't thrilled with the prospect at all.

Sure, my dream of being a doctor had died a quick death. And, yes, the idea of being a cop had been in the back of my mind since childhood.

But more recently, my plan had been to finish college and become an FBI agent. Yet when I had looked into all the federal law enforcement agencies – FBI, Secret Service, CIA, etc. – they all seemed to want lawyers and accountants and experts on foreign languages. Or they wanted men and women with a college degree and three years of military experience.

So on Sept. 2, 1980, with very little fanfare and not exactly brimming with enthusiasm, I reported to the police academy on East 20th St. in Manhattan.

It would turn out to be the best move I ever made.

Unless you consider that, 22 years later, it would lead to my personal destruction.

2

"The Last Great American Heroes"

At the risk of understatement, it's fair to say I came to the police academy with a *major* attitude problem.

"This job sucks," became my mantra.

I said it dozens of times a day. I said it out loud. And I said it to whoever would listen.

I was 20 years old, thought I knew everything and was supremely bitter about having to leave college. Plus from the moment I started at the academy, it seemed that the instructors were intent on busting my balls, either for the sheer thrill of it or because it afforded a break from the tedium of their miserable, ho-hum lives.

Now, not only were they telling me I had to shave every day, I had to shave "close," which no one seemed able to fully describe or quantify.

And the ball-busting didn't stop there. Our uniform consisted of navy blue pants, light blue shirt, clip-on black tie and black shoes, which looked about as fashionable as it sounds. I'd shine my shoes to a high gloss, only to have an instructor stare at them as if I'd just chased weasels through a swamp.

"Those shoes look like shit," he'd say. "I'm writing you up."

I understood it was all part of the game. It was what they did in an effort to instill discipline in the new cops and make them part of a team.

But I wasn't in any mood for it. Just a few weeks earlier, I'd been a college hotshot, an All-American frat boy – at least in my own mind – with unlimited potential. Now I wasn't sure what I was.

This is stupid, I told myself over and over again those first few weeks at the academy. *I hate this place.*

But ever so slowly, my perspective began to change.

For one thing, I became good friends with a core group of smart guys in our class who'd had successful jobs, but for various reasons now wanted to be cops. And because I was in such great shape from football two-a-days at Rochester, I enjoyed all the physical aspects of my new life.

In many ways, academy training was like going to college. You worked out every day, ran, boxed, learned self-defense, how to use a nightstick and how to handcuff people. You took college level classes in political science, social science and law.

Except . . . you also visited extremely weird places.

Like the morgue.

Policemen see death on a regular basis, of course. So to ensure that a rookie cop wouldn't react to the sight of his or her first corpse by panicking or passing out in the street, new recruits were acclimated to stiffs amid the cheerful ambience of the mortuary and autopsy rooms at famed Bellevue Hospital.

I thought I'd have no problems handling the morgue.

Years earlier, when I was 15 and on one of my long commutes to Brooklyn Tech, I had seen the gruesome results of a mob hit. Changing buses one day, I saw a bunch of cops surrounding a roped-off car, where a crowd had quickly gathered.

In the front seat of the sedan was the body of a man who'd been shot in the head. He was the first dead person I had ever seen outside a funeral home, and the sight had not greatly disturbed me.

But apparently it hadn't prepared me for the assault to the senses that was the Bellevue morgue, either.

I was OK when we toured the mortuary and they began opening stainless-steel drawers on which dead people were arrayed in various poses.

But the autopsy room came as a total shock.

Under brilliant white lights, against a backdrop of more dazzling whiteness reflecting off the walls, were a row of bodies, all in various states of dismemberment.

One man's chest was being cracked open. Another man's skull was being sawed off. Yet another body was being sewn back together with a giant needle. Livers were being extracted and brains were being measured on scales like so many slabs of meat at the supermarket.

And at each of these tables, streams of blood were flowing down big built-in metal grooves leading to collection buckets on the floor.

I thought I was going to pass out.

I had to get out of there. So I bolted for the door. And it took me quite a few minutes to regain my composure. (After the training session, we all went out for pizza, which I found to be funny. You're seeing all this blood and all these organs, intestines and tissue everywhere – and then you go out for a large sausage and pepperoni pie? I guess we were becoming inured to the sight of gore already. Either that or we were all sick puppies.)

Within weeks of entering the academy, though, the former Mr. Bad Attitude was all-in on the cop life.

I remember being on a date with an old high school flame – we were headed to the movies – when, in the middle of Flatlands Avenue, I saw two guys beating the hell out of another guy with baseball bats.

I was still in the academy, but we had already gotten our guns and shields. So I was armed and had a badge.

Damn, I thought, *I can't ignore this! I'm a police officer now. My days of driving past things like this are over.*

So I stopped my car and got out, drawing my weapon. Just then a police car with a couple of older cops pulled up. To this day I don't know if someone called them or they happened by on patrol.

But the three of us broke up the assault, and we all went back to the precinct house with the bad guys. ("Sorry, no movie tonight," I had to tell my date. "Take the car home.")

"OK, kid, here's your collar," the two older cops told me back at the station house.

Wait, they were giving *me* the collar?

I had never made an arrest before! I had no idea what to do.

So I called my father, whose first reaction was: "Oh, geez, what the hell did you do?" But he met me at the precinct, helped me with the initial processing and accompanied me to Central Booking for further processing of the two perps.

By this point, the two older cops were long gone, thrilled to have avoided the burdensome paperwork and next-day court appearance that comes with being the arresting officer. The two, I would learn, had a reputation for being lazy cops. It was my first up-close-and-personal look at that particular sub-section of the force – although not, unfortunately, my last.

Six months after entering the academy, I was part of a class of 500 rookies who became full-fledged police officers during graduation ceremonies at Brooklyn College. My family threw a big party for me afterward and friends and cousins showered me with gifts that included things like a shoulder holster, which provided a new dose of reality.

It made me realize I'd be carrying a gun every day for the rest of my working life. Nevertheless, I felt very proud of getting through the academy and excited about starting my new career.

Here I was officially a New York City police officer and I had yet to turn 21. Less than a year earlier, my biggest concern on the weekends was: which keg party should I go to tonight and what girls would be there?

Now, in less than 48 hours, Eddie Norris would be carrying a gun and badge and patrolling Times Square, tasked with the awesome responsibility of keeping the masses safe from the unsavory army of lowlifes who preyed there day in and day out.

So it was that on the evening of Jan. 27, 1981, I reported to the Midtown North precinct for my very first shift, 5 p.m. to 1 a.m.

Some 40 rookie cops from three precincts – Midtown North, Midtown South and the 17th – joined me at that roll call. We were turned out by a lieutenant named Lou Anemone.

Anemone cut an impressive figure. He had a rep as a cop who could walk the walk. He had worked everywhere, all the toughest precincts in the city, including Harlem at the height of the BLA cop-killings.

He was trim, dark-haired and only in his early 30's, but looked totally squared away in his uniform, with a rack of medals on his chest so shiny they could cause retinal damage.

"You guys are the last great American heroes!" he thundered, proceeding to give us a terrific motivational talk about what it meant to be a police officer and how much good we were doing for society.

I want to be like that guy, I thought, as I was driven to my post on 42nd St., between 7th and 8th Avenues.

That first night as a full-fledged cop, I felt proud, excited and awestruck at being in Times Square in uniform and carrying a gun, with people looking at me for help. You become a magnet for people with problems. In that teeming acre of concrete, with thousands of people passing my post by the hour, I was a reassuring presence for the wide-eyed tourists making their first visit to the Big Apple, and a source of consternation for all the bad guys bent on ruining that visit.

Nothing terribly crazy happened on that first shift. At one point I was sent to provide back-up at a nearby demonstration. This being New York, of course, a demonstration was not at all unusual – New Yorkers will demonstrate over getting a bad pastrami sandwich if you let them.

The only other noteworthy thing that happened was that I responded to a radio dispatcher's 10-13 call, the signal code that means "officer needs assistance."

I took off sprinting to the location of the call, which was a couple of blocks away. But when I arrived breathless and red-faced, there were already a bunch of police cars there, lights flashing, and the other cops were looking at me like: *Kid, what the hell are you doing here?*

It would prove to be an unfounded call. As I was to learn, "10-13" calls come in all night from the dispatchers. If you hear a cop screaming "10-13!" over the radio, you know that's different. That's *serious.* But store owners call these in all night long if, for instance, they want you to toss a sleeping homeless guy from their establishment or break up a fight.

Even the crooks themselves will call in a "10-13" to create a diversion and have the police respond to one part of town while they're pulling off a crime in another part.

Being in Times Square, an area saturated with cops, I probably shouldn't have responded to that "10-13" in the first place. I was a little embarrassed that I did. But the veteran cops already on the scene didn't make me feel like a jerk. They just counseled me on why my response was unnecessary.

My first days on the job were with a training officer, and they continued to be exciting, even if the work had its mundane aspects.

Basically, your night consisted of moving along the drunks who were causing disturbances and the shitheads who were trying to intimidate people and disrupt businesses. Often, these lowlifes would go into one of the numerous pizza and gyro places, take food and refuse to pay. Or they'd threaten to come back and kill the owner if he did anything about it.

Needless to say, these business owners loved having cops patronizing their joints. They'd feed us and take care of us. In turn, we'd respond quickly whenever there was some skell who needed to be grabbed by the back of the neck and tossed out.

In the summer of '81, I was transferred to Midtown South, which is exactly where I wanted to go. They had a big sign in the station house proclaiming: "Busiest precinct in the world." And from the volume of crime being handled there every day, that was no exaggeration.

By now I had seen plenty of dead people. I'd seen people shot to death, stabbed to death and run over by a subway train. I'd seen people who had keeled over from heart attacks. So when I was assigned to watch over a DOA at the Hotel Carter, it seemed like pretty cut-and-dried duty.

The Carter was an aging, 24-story hotel just off Times Square with a reputation as a hangout for thieves, hookers and all sorts of other underworld denizens. (In the early 2000's, it would achieve the unenviable distinction of being ranked the dirtiest hotel in America. TripAdvisor warned its clients of the Carter's bedbug infestation and generally "unsafe" conditions, the main one apparently being that you could get murdered there in a heartbeat.)

The dead person in this case was a black male in his early 30's. He'd been shot right between the eyes. When I got to his room, he was stark naked and laying half-off the bed, blood leaking from the hole in his head.

Now that all the crime scene technicians had left, my job was to watch over the stiff until the medical examiner came to collect him. I knew this could take all day. So to kill time, I'd brought along a paperback book aptly entitled "No One Here Gets Out Alive," the biography of the Doors charismatic lead singer, Jim Morrison.

For an hour, I stood and leaned against the door in this tiny room, trying to get comfortable. Finally I thought: *Fuck this. No one's coming to get this guy for hours.* With that, I slid into bed next to the corpse and continued happily reading for the rest of the afternoon.

The irony of the whole scene wasn't lost on me.

Here was a young cop who, just a year earlier, thought he was going to pass out in the morgue. Yet now he was comfortable enough with death to be reading in a bed next to a naked murder victim with blood dribbling from his forehead.

As I was to learn quickly, there were times on the job when you could go from the ridiculous to the sublime in the course of a single shift.

Not long after baby-sitting the stiff at the Hotel Carter, my partner Dan Mullin and I were asked to "clean up the block" on 41ˢᵗ St. near the Nederlander Theatre.

This was because the great singer and actress Lena Horne was appearing there in a one-woman Broadway show called "The Lady and Her Music." And the area around the theatre was dark and desolate at night, with all manner of pickpockets, thieves, panhandlers, junkies and hookers ready to waylay anyone stupid enough to cut through on their way to the Port Authority bus terminal.

"Clean up the block" was a police euphemism for "Get these scumbags out of here any way you have to."

At first, Dan and I tried to kindly ask the more shady citizens of 41ˢᵗ St. to relocate their "businesses" elsewhere. But if that didn't work, we were forced to give them an "attitude adjustment" and convince them they weren't coming back to the block any time in the near future.

Pretty soon, with all the riff-raff gone, the area around the Nederlander looked much more inviting. The theater people and patrons were grateful for our efforts. And, as it turned out, they weren't the only ones.

One night, as I was stood outside the theatre in a driving rainstorm not long after the show let out, a cab pulled up to the curb. In jumped Lena Horne. Seconds later, she was followed by another musical legend, Harry Belafonte, the "King of Calypso" and crooner of the "Banana Boat Song" himself.

The cab took off and went about 10 yards before the cabbie abruptly slammed on the brakes. Out jumped Belafonte into the pouring rain. Walking over to me, he shook my hand and said: "Thank you for all you do."

Inside the cab, I could see Lena Horne smiling and waving, too. Then Belafonte jumped back in and the cab took off again, leaving a young cop dazzled by the classy gesture he had just witnessed from two show business icons.

Yet the old line about race car drivers, soldiers and cops – that their work involves hours of boredom punctuated by moments of sheer terror – definitely proved to be true. Especially when I was involved in my first shootout.

I'd been on the job two years and was working plainclothes with my partner Dan Mullin in the Midtown South Anti-Crime unit. It was a blistering hot July 3 and we were driving a fake medallion cab around the city.

No, check that, *I* was driving the fake cab, because Dan was from Long Island and couldn't stand driving in heavy traffic. On this day, Midtown was even more of a traffic-choked nightmare than usual, with everyone scrambling to get to Penn Station and out of town for the holiday weekend.

We had just gotten in the cab when we heard a male cop's frantic voice over the radio: "10-13! 10-13! Shots fired!"

This one was for real. Some two hundred yards in front of us, a man and woman had just robbed a furrier and jumped into a getaway car, which was now stuck in traffic. Detectives having lunch at a nearby Irish pub had heard the call and confronted the robbers, who had shot at them through the car's window.

One of the detectives had been hit in the neck. Now the scene was chaos, with hundreds of people screaming and running in panic, and police converging on the car.

We jumped out of our cab and ran to the getaway car with guns drawn. The police were returning fire, but I couldn't get off a shot because there was a cop between me and the car. Suddenly, I saw the male suspect, who was in the passenger seat, get hit and slump over. We could immediately see he was dead – brain matter was oozing from the wound.

I ran around to the driver's side, stuck my gun in the woman's ear and dragged her out of the car.

"GET YOUR HANDS OFF ME, MOTHERFUCKER!" she

kept screaming. "CANT YOU SEE I'M SHOT?!"

She sure was. She had a couple of .38-caliber slugs in her, but she was still mean as a snake, cursing me the whole time. (Later, I would be told that the detective who was shot was rushed to Bellevue and would survive. But the getaway driver with the cheerful manner and charming vocabulary would end up paralyzed for life.)

As for me, after the first shooting incident of my police career, I sat on the curb in stunned silence for several minutes, numb but also happy to be alive. My hands weren't shaking. I hadn't felt frightened. But replaying it all in my head felt like I was watching myself in a movie.

Interspersed between the routine parts of the job and the adrenalized moments when your life could hang in the balance, there were also moments of dark humor. Some were so delicious as to be unforgettable.

On patrol in uniform one night, Dan and I spotted a suspicious-looking car with New Jersey license plates parked in an alley at the end of a block.

Shining our flashlights inside, we were treated – if that's the word – to the sight of a teenager behind the wheel getting a blowjob from a woman in the passenger seat. Two other boys, who looked to be high school age, were in the back seat.

We ordered all four out of the car. The hooker, whom we immediately recognized as a local, seemed unperturbed. But the three kids were practically hyperventilating, no doubt contemplating the cosmic shit-storm that was about to descend on them for soliciting a prostitute.

Not only were they now entertaining visions of being carted off to jail and sexually violated by all manner of hardened criminals looking for fresh meat, but it was a sure bet mommy and daddy back in Jersey weren't going to be thrilled with junior's new hobby of patronizing streetwalkers, either.

Yet the fact was, Dan and I had no intention of making a prostitution arrest. That was just not something that a uniform cop would do.

If you came back to the station house with a hooker in handcuffs, your bosses would be furious. For one thing, now you'd be off the street for the night filling out paperwork. Plus you'd have to go to court with the hooker the next day. And finally your supervisors would assume you made the arrest just to get some easy overtime. That's why prostitution arrests were mainly left to the Public Morals Division.

But if Dan and I weren't going to bust anyone here, at least we were going to get a few laughs out of the whole thing.

"Look," I said to the hooker, "we'll make you a deal. Either you're gonna get locked up, or you're gonna show them and I'll let you go."

The kids looked puzzled. The hooker smoothed her slinky red dress. Then she patted her towering blonde wig, which looked like something out of the Dolly Parton Collection, and laughed nervously.

"C'mon, I don't have time for this!" I barked. "Show them or you're going to jail! Your choice!"

With a shrug, the hooker pulled up her dress, pulled down her panties – and out fell the biggest cock you've ever seen outside an NBA locker room.

Two of the kids looked like they were about to puke. The third started to laugh.

"What's so funny?" I demanded, shining my flashlight in his face.

"It's just . . . I didn't get a turn with her," he said, still giggling.

He sounded eternally grateful for that, too. I always wondered if the kid made it back to Jersey alive, or whether his buddies dumped his battered body somewhere in the Meadowlands to preserve their mortifying secret.

Dan and I chuckled as the kids took off in their car and the street-walker tottered away unsteadily on six-inch heels, off to find another lonely and horny john in the city that never sleeps.

Watching her disappear into the night, I had something of an epiphany.

God, I thought, *I'm really starting to love this job.*

3

"Better Get a Good Mouthpiece"

In December of 1984, at the age of 24, I was promoted to sergeant and assigned to the 13th Precinct in the affluent Gramercy Park area of Manhattan.

Looking back on it now, I was *way* too young to be a sergeant. But I had aced the test and had just passed my three-year anniversary on the force, making me eligible for the position.

Right away, I made all the classic mistakes of a newbie suddenly thrust in a leadership role. You try to be everybody's buddy. You're a great guy until the first day you turn somebody down for a day off. Suddenly – *Boom!* – you're a scumbag.

You want to get close to the guys you're working with, figuring it will make you a better supervisor. So you drink with them. You hang out with them. You want to be their friend. But the fact is, you have to be their boss, not their buddy. And the stark realization of this will quickly slap you in the face.

At the Thanksgiving Day parade the following year, I spent hours looking for two senior patrolmen who had been assigned to a post near Macy's department store. I was there to sign their memo books – we called it "giving them a scratch" – to make sure they were on the job and doing what they were supposed to do.

Except . . . guess what? These two knuckleheads were nowhere to be found.

I couldn't get them on the radio, either. Now I was getting madder and madder. They were obviously goofing off somewhere. By the time they showed up at the end of their tour with some lame excuse, I was steaming.

So I wrote them up – reported them on a command discipline form. Now it was up to the captain to decide their punishment. But because they were older guys with 30-some years on the job, the captain didn't punish them at all.

Instead, they were given a slap on the wrist – which made *me* look like a total jerk. That day I made a mental note to myself: you need to take care of this stuff on your own. In the future, if this sort of thing happened, I'd find ways to punish the dipshits myself.

Maybe I'd assign them to watch over so many dead bodies they'd think they were in a war zone. Or I'd take them out of a radio car and make them walk a beat again. Or every time another precinct needed extra officers for some particularly crappy assignment, I'd send these two lazy bastards. If it wasn't against union rules, I'd have 'em clean up horseshit after a parade.

My days as a sergeant also marked the first time I got in trouble for using excessive force.

This was after I'd been transferred to the 6th Precinct in the West Village. One day, I was working a Spanish-American pride festival when I spotted a big muscular guy, shirtless and crazy-looking. He was storming up and down the block, muttering to himself, snatching food from the vendors and scaring the hell out of everybody.

I tried to grab him by the arm and talk to him, but this did not go well. He pushed me into a store window. I bounced off the glass, grabbed my radio and called for an ambulance to pick up an emotionally-disturbed person. I also called in a "10-85," which basically means a cop needs assistance, although not as urgently as a "10-13."

My struggle with the deranged man continued. He was fighting me and sweaty as hell, and it was hard to get a grip on him. Finally, when he charged at another officer who had just arrived on the scene,

I took out my nightstick and whacked him across the neck.

He fell like a tree, toppling face down on the sidewalk, leaking blood everywhere. We managed to handcuff him and get him into the ambulance strapped to a gurney, but he still resisted us all the way, biting, spitting and head-butting.

Soon enough, we'd learn he had either escaped or been discharged from Creedmoor, the notorious psychiatric hospital in Queens. And right away, people started coming out of the woodwork, eager to testify that I had been too brutal with the man.

None of this was particularly surprising. Greenwich Village was maybe the most left-wing neighborhood in New York City, and many of the residents made no secret of their antipathy toward the police.

Also, it was not unusual to be hit with an excessive force charge if you were an aggressive police officer intent on doing your job well.

People wanted to believe that cops were so well-trained they could subdue a raving 220-pound man by grabbing his pinkie and doing some kind of sick ju-jitsu move to drop him to his knees. This was a complete fantasy.

Hell, no one – not even the Navy SEALS – is *that* well-trained.

The fact was, this unhinged man was intent on hurting another person. And he *would* have if I hadn't hit him with my nightstick as I did.

Nevertheless, I was ordered to appear before the Civilian Complaint Review Board, where I told my story and was promptly exonerated, to my tremendous relief.

My next assignment was a stint in Brooklyn South narcotics, supervising buy-and-busts in the streets, parks and nightclubs.

Narcotics was wildly exciting to me. It was dangerous, unpredictable work, but important, too. It was also unlike anything I had ever done before. We wore disguises, listened in on wire taps, hung out in discos all night long to observe dozens of furtive – and not-so-furtive – drug transactions taking place.

One case in particular would stick with me for years. We had been buying heroin and cocaine from this one particular group of dealers for many months. In fact, we'd infiltrated the ring so successfully – hanging with them, joking with them, drinking with them – that the dealers came to regard us as fast friends and not simply as business associates.

On the last day of the operation, when it came time to take everyone down, we fanned out in teams and hit the various locations of the dealers simultaneously. This way they couldn't warn one another when an arrest was made.

I went with an officer named Brian McCarthy to the house of one dealer, who was in his early 20's and still living with his parents. Brian had been buying dope off the man for months, and he greeted us with a big smile.

For all the man knew, Brian was there looking to buy some more stuff and I was one of Brian's partners, which seemed perfectly reasonable.

When we arrived, the dealer's mother was in the kitchen making pasta for dinner. We talked to him in the living room. After a hasty greeting, Brian quietly informed him that we were police officers.

The guy was incredulous. He managed a nervous grin.

What?! You guys are cops? No way!

But within seconds, it dawned on him that his life was about to go completely off the rails.

You never know what a drug dealer will do in moments like this. Some try to bolt. Some try to fight you. Some whip out a gun or a knife.

To make sure he didn't try anything stupid, I grabbed him by the arm. My gun was already pointing at him in my coat pocket.

"Listen," I said in a low voice, "if you do anything stupid, I'll kill you right in front of your mother. Think about that."

The kid turned pale. The grin was gone.

"How about you tell your mom you're leaving for a few minutes?" I went on.

The guy looked at me. Then he looked at Brian. Now the light seemed to go out of his eyes and his shoulders sagged. Finally he nodded.

"All right, ma, I'll see you!" he yelled into the kitchen. "I'm going out for a while."

We took him outside and cuffed him and brought him to the station house. All across this part of Brooklyn, the same scene was being repeated over and over: dazed-looking drug dealers were being hauled off to jail by their former "buddies," many of the dope peddlers still convinced this was some kind of gigantic crazy prank being played on them.

This was the first time that the so-called "war on drugs" really hit home with me.

This is serious, I remember thinking. *These guys are in their early 20's. And they're going to jail for a long time, maybe decades. They'll be middle-aged men when they get out.*

Over time, I would come to believe the war on drugs was folly, a huge waste of time and money. The flow of drugs is impossible to stop. And did we learn nothing from the Prohibition era?

Didn't we learn that if people want to get drunk, they're going to find a way to get drunk? And if they want to get high, they'll get high? We can't legislate morality, it's that simple. And even though we've tried for hundreds of years, it's insane to think we'll ever be successful.

But on this chilly fall night in Brooklyn, it somehow seemed as if we were doing God's work, ridding the streets of dangerous people and fulfilling our vow to keep the peace.

After narcotics, my next stop was the 7th Precinct detective squad on Manhattan's Lower East Side. Here the work was even more interesting, in my opinion – and more meaningful, too. I lived for the days when I got to break the news to a grieving widow or mother that we'd arrested the lowlife who'd killed her husband or son.

Then, when I least expected it, another bombshell hit.

Right after I took the test to become a lieutenant – and finished no. 5 on the list – Michigan Congressman John Conyers, then the chairman of the House Subcommittee on Criminal Justice, opened a 17-month inquiry on racism and police brutality in New York and other large cities.

And the NYPD, because it has no balls, caved in immediately to the publicity-seeking politician.

Instead of standing up for its officers and saying no, fuck you, we've investigated these cases ourselves and there's no pattern of brutality, the NYPD re-opened 50 old excessive-force cases.

And guess whose case was included?

Bingo.

Just like that, the bogus charge that I had brutalized a disturbed man in the Village went from "unsubstantiated and exonerated" to: "You're going to trial, kid. You and the rest of these rogue cops. Better get yourself a good mouthpiece."

Which is exactly what I did.

Faced with criminal prosecution and the chance I might lose my job altogether, I was forced to hire an expensive lawyer, instead of the hacks the department routinely provided gratis. My trial, a formal, nerve-wracking affair, was held at police headquarters.

Thankfully, the unhinged man I'd arrested was never found by the time the case went to court. And the witnesses summoned by the prosecution gave so many conflicting versions of what had happened that the judge became exasperated at one point and shouted: "Would you please make up your mind on *one* story?!"

Still, the tension was high until the very end, when I was again cleared of any wrong-doing.

The only bit of levity I remember came when I bragged to my lawyer, Rosemary Carroll, that I had just aced the NYPD's lieutenant's test.

"Hey, I'm no. 5 on the list!" I told her. "And something like 3,000 sergeants took the test. What do you think of that?"

Rosemary, a tough Irish attorney married to a Jewish judge,

quickly shot me down.

"Yeah, that's really good," she said. "For a Jew, you're about average. For an Irishman, you're a fucking genius."

Me? A genius? Hot damn!

I wondered if that could be noted on my official transcript.

4

The Assassination of Meir Kahane

My promotion to lieutenant in November of 1989 was bitter-sweet. The good news: I was now in charge of the 7th Precinct detective squad. The bad news: I was still in the 7th Precinct.

The 7th, right by the Williamsburg Bridge on the Lower East Side of Manhattan, was a real shithole back then. It was infested with heroin and every other drug, and sometimes it seemed as if the streets were owned by vacant-eyed zombies and lowlifes at all hours of the day and night.

The precinct house was on the aptly-named Pitt Street. You couldn't make this up.

This is the kind of neighborhood it was: on Halloween, another detective and I were headed out to dinner when we heard a series of gunshots: *pop! pop! pop! pop!* We heard over the radio that the uniforms were chasing a suspect in the shooting. We joined the pursuit and the guy was quickly caught.

It turned out that somebody had been throwing eggs at him. So this genius had picked up a brand-new Heckler & Koch 9-mm pistol and decided to murder the egg-thrower. He attempted this by firing wildly into the street, not exactly caring whether he might cut down an innocent bystander – or maybe 10 of them – in the process.

Needless to say, when I was offered the command of another detective squad, this one at the 17th Precinct, I leapt at the opportunity.

The 17th was in mid-town Manhattan and considered one of the two or three nicest precincts in the city.

Some of the wealthiest people in the country had homes in the neighborhood, including Henry Kissinger, Katherine Hepburn, fashion designer Bill Blass, cabaret singer Bobby Short and Mets' first baseman Keith Hernandez.

I was barely 30 years old. Compared to the 7th, it was like I'd died and gone to heaven. Everywhere you looked there were terrific restaurants, beautiful women and interesting people doing the most interesting things.

On the other hand, I didn't exactly have a chance to ease into the job.

No, after my very first day as the commanding officer of the 17th squad, just as I sat down to dinner in my Staten Island condo, the phone rang. Calling was Eileen Brennan, the woman I was replacing as head of the 17th's detectives.

"Eddie," she said, "we have a shooting."

What? I thought. *A shooting? Nobody gets shot in that neighborhood!*

Which was mostly true. Maybe there were one or two murders a year on average. And those were often, ahem, "business-related," like when mob boss John Gotti had fellow Mafiosi Paul Castellano whacked in front of Sparks Steak House a few years earlier.

"A guy's dead in a hotel," Eileen continued. "It's a rabbi. Meir something or other . . ."

"Meir Kahane?" I asked.

"Yeah, that's him," she said.

Holy shit! Oh, I knew all about Meir Kahane.

Kahane, 58, was the founder of the ultra-conservative Jewish Defense League. He was a fiery orator who had called for the expulsion of all Arabs from Israel and the mass emigration of U.S. Jews to their biblical homeland, presumably to save them from a "second

Holocaust."

He called Arabs "jackals," pushed for laws that would bar Arabs and Jews from having sex and organized "defense squads" to patrol Jewish neighborhoods and beat the shit out of anyone deemed a possible threat.

Hmmm, I thought, *who would want to kill a sweetheart like that?*

After hanging up with Eileen, I packed a duffle bag with a couple of days' worth of clothes and drove straight to the crime scene at the Marriott East Side hotel.

What had happened was this: some 90 minutes earlier, Kahane had finished another of his rabidly anti-Arab speeches to a fervent group of his followers in one of the hotel conference rooms.

He had left the podium and was shaking hands, posing for pictures and signing copies of his book, when a man named El Sayyid Nosair walked up behind him.

Nosair, Egyptian by birth but now an American citizen, was wearing a yarmulke and posing as a Sephardic Jew. Suddenly, he produced a .357 magnum and squeezed off two shots that struck Kahane in the neck.

Amid the screams and confusion that followed, Nosair had tried to flee.

"It's Allah's will!" he reportedly shouted.

When an elderly follower of Kahane's had tried to stop him, Nosair had shot the man in the leg before bolting out the hotel's front door.

Once outside, as we would learn later, he had expected to jump in a get-away cab driven by one of his confederates, a hulking, red-headed Egyptian named Mahmoud Abouhalima.

But the cab had been prevented from parking in front of the hotel by police who were in charge of security on traffic-choked Lexington Avenue. Confused and panic-stricken now, Nosair had jumped in another cab by mistake, then leaped out when the driver slammed on the brakes.

Fleeing the scene, Nosair had come across a uniformed U.S. Postal police officer named Carlos Acosta. Spotting Nosair's gun, Acosta had drawn his own weapon. Nosair had shot first, the bullet grazing Acosta's bulletproof vest. Acosta staggered, but was able to return fire, hitting Nosair in the neck.

Nosair toppled to the sidewalk, blood pouring from his wound. Thus ended the dramatic chase, in a wail of ambulance sirens as the assassin was rushed to Bellevue Hospital. Ironically, he would arrive shortly after another ambulance screamed up to the ER entrance, this one carrying the lifeless body of Kahane.

Nosair, though, would survive.

When we went through his pockets, we found a wallet and papers listing prominent Jewish politicians in the New York area. It looked for all the world like a hit list. I then sent detectives to the address we had from his driver's license, which was an apartment in Jersey City, N.J.

By the time the detectives got there, it was around 1 in the morning. Yet after just a few knocks, the door was answered by a tall, strapping Egyptian with bright red hair. Another Egyptian man – identified as Mohammed Salameh – was also there.

Neither appeared to have been sleeping. And neither seemed particularly surprised at finding police on their doorstep at that hour.

In short order, both men admitted to knowing Nosair, but said he did not live there anymore. Both also said they were cab drivers. And both disclosed that they'd been in the vicinity of the Marriott hotel at the time of the Kahane shooting.

So what we had – for all intents and purposes – were the getaway car drivers. Since the NYPD had no jurisdiction in New Jersey, we got them to "voluntarily" come back to the 17th Precinct for questioning. And as soon as they crossed the Hudson River, they were arrested.

Not long after, my detectives managed to find out where Nosair had been living, which was in a rental house in Cliffside Park, N.J., just across the George Washington Bridge. We obtained a warrant, searched the house and came up with a veritable treasure trove of information.

What were brought back to me were two file cabinets full of all kinds of documents, most written in Arabic. There were obvious bomb-making manuals. There were maps and 8x10 photos of city landmarks such as Police Headquarters, St. Patrick's Cathedral, the Brooklyn Bridge, the World Trade Center and FBI headquarters.

In a black-and-white marble composition book, there were notes in Arabic and drawings of a city street with little symbols of cars blocking intersections. (I thought the drawings might have something to do with an armored car stickup Nosair and his associates were planning. But they would later turn out to be related to a plot to kill Egyptian president Hosni Mubarak on his visit to New York.)

Finally, there were also classified U.S. documents as well as training manuals from the Army Special Warfare Center and School at Fort Bragg, the huge military base in North Carolina.

It was all eye-popping stuff. My head was spinning as I wrestled with the myriad implications of what we'd found.

The next morning, I headed down to headquarters at One Police Plaza for a big briefing with the department's chief of detectives, Joseph Borelli.

Borelli was a man who favored cardigan sweaters and curved smoking pipes right out of a Sherlock Holmes movie. The whole effect made him seem avuncular and low-key. He was a nice enough guy. But some thought he was still living off his rep as the head of the task force that had tracked down the notorious "Son of Sam" serial killer, David Berkowitz, in the summer of 1977.

Arrayed around the table in the big conference room were various police commanders, FBI agents and Joint Terrorism Task Force agents.

As the lieutenant in charge of the case, I filled everyone in on what we had on Nosair and the Kahane killing so far.

When I was done, Borelli said: "Eddie, can you tell me this guy acted alone?"

"Of course not," I said.

I told him about the two suspects, Abouhalima and Salameh, who were under arrest, charged with being the getaway drivers. The shooter, obviously, was also under arrest. And now we had reams of drawings, photos, maps and classified U.S. documents taken from the shooter's house.

"I have *something* here," I told Borelli. "I don't exactly know what it is. But it's big."

It quickly became apparent that the chief of detectives did not share my viewpoint.

"Oh, you shut up!" he barked. "You handle the murder OK?" He pointed at the FBI agents across the table. "*They* handle the conspiracies."

I was stunned. My Irish temper flared as I sat down.

"This is bullshit!" I whispered to my captain, Mike Gardner. "What are we gonna do?"

Gardner shrugged and pointed to Borelli.

"You want to tell him again?" he asked.

No, definitely not.

As angry as I was, Joe Borelli was a three-star chief and I was a young lieutenant. And the police department was still a paramilitary organization. The chief tells you to shut up, you shut up.

I was steaming, but I wasn't stupid. No way was I going to get in a shouting match with a well-respected superior and risk derailing my career completely.

So it was that later that morning, at a packed press conference, Borelli would insist that Kahane's murder was the result of a "lone deranged gunman."

"He didn't seem to be part of a conspiracy or a terrorist organization," the chief of detectives would add for emphasis.

Unfortunately, there were more shocking developments in store for me and my detectives after the chief met the media.

While I was out to lunch that day, the feds came into our squad room and removed the file cabinets containing the damning evidence seized from Nosair's house. We would never learn where the files ended up, either.

This was followed by another jaw-dropping event: Abouhalima and Salameh were released from custody, on the grounds there was not enough evidence to hold them.

Again, I was livid.

Ordinarily in policing, if you have enough probable cause to lock someone up, they're locked up and *stay* locked up. And you let the district attorney and judge sort out the details of the case.

Maybe later on it turns out you don't have enough probable cause to hold the suspect or suspects. But there was no question that the quick release of the two Egyptians in such a high-profile case was highly unusual, to say the least.

Over the years, historians combing the Nosair case have advanced a number of theories for Joe Borelli's reluctance to dig deeper into the circumstances surrounding the Kahane murder.

In "Two Seconds Under the World," a book about the developments that led to the first World Trade Center bombing in 1993, *Newsday* reporters Jim Dwyer, David Kocieniewski, Diedre Murphy and Peg Tyre wrote: "There hadn't been any political assassinations in New York in more than a decade and Borelli didn't want one on his watch."

And in the exhaustively-researched 2002 book "The Cell: Inside the 9/11 Plot and Why the FBI and CIA Failed to Stop It," one of the authors, John Miller, wrote: ". . . (Borelli) was a loyal general, not a revolutionary, and the prevailing theory in the NYPD was 'Don't make waves.' . . .So in the Nosair case, when Chief Borelli turned a blind eye to the obvious, he was only remaining true to the culture of the NYPD.

"The thinking was, Don't take a high-profile homicide case that could be stamped 'Solved' and turn it into an unsolved conspiracy. To do so would create a lot of extra work."

Whatever the reason for Borelli's stance, it would leave me irate and disillusioned for years.

Our investigation into Kahane's death continued, but I was soon transferred to the Department of Investigation, the watchdog agency that roots out corruption among police, city employees and elected officials. This was considered a prestigious assignment and a big step up the career ladder.

In my heart, though, I would always believe El Sayyid Nosair and his accomplices were part of a vast and dangerous conspiracy bent on doing irreparable harm to this country – and that the NYPD missed a golden opportunity to stop them.

Unfortunately, subsequent events would prove me right.

On a cold February afternoon in 1993, I was in my DOI office in lower Manhattan when I heard what sounded like an explosion.

At first, we thought nothing of it. We thought it was a subway transformer exploding, which happened from time to time.

But within minutes, I got a call from Inspector Don Morse of the detective bureau.

"Eddie, we gotta talk," he said. "They just bombed the World Trade Center."

History would record that six people were killed and over 1,000 injured when the 1,200-pound bomb, planted in a Ryder truck in a parking garage beneath the North Tower, exploded.

Six suspects would ultimately be convicted of the plot. The mastermind, a Kuwaiti named Ramzi Yousef, would be found to have spent time in an al-Qaeda training camp in Afghanistan. The bombing, he would claim, was done in retaliation for the suffering the Palestinian people had endured at the hands of U.S.-backed Israel.

But the names of two of the convicted terrorists would haunt me for a long, long time.

Mohammad Salameh would be identified as the man who rented the Ryder truck. And Mahmoud Abouhalima, the big red-headed

Egyptian, would be seen by witnesses with Salameh at a storage facility in Jersey City where the explosives were allegedly prepared.

To this day, the idea that I was sitting on three major suspects and important information in 1990 that might have prevented future attacks on this country – and that no one acted on it – makes me sick.

"Many officials," the authors of "The Cell" wrote, "Norris among them, have since claimed that the (Nosair) files provided a virtual road map to future terrorist acts, including the 1993 World Trade Center bombing. Along with the military documents, the bomb manuals, and the diagrams and photos of New York landmarks, the Nosair papers contained a manifesto exhorting his associates to topple the 'tall buildings of which Americans are so proud.'"

In a later aside, "The Cell" co-author John Miller added:

"Nosair turned out to be the pioneer of a new kind of terrorism, the first to act out the malicious ideology of a rogue strain of Islam that would eventually seek to eviscerate the American way of life. More than a symbol, he would prove to be, even as he sat behind bars, an instigator and source of inspiration for other like-minded militants. In fact, in any attempt to understand the events of Sept. 11, 2001, it makes sense to begin with El Sayyid Nosair.

"That's where the law enforcement aspect of the Sept. 11 story began, and where American law enforcement agencies first revealed themselves to be institutionally ill-equipped for the war this new enemy had brought to U.S. shores."

All I can say to that is: Amen.

5

"MC-BEE! MC-BEE!"

New York in the early 1990's was dangerous and dirty, a chilling portrait of a once-proud metropolis in steep decline.

Crime was out of control. Under the administration of genial, dapper and largely-ineffective mayor David Dinkins, the number of murders, assaults, robberies, burglaries and car thefts had skyrocketed.

Racial tensions, especially between the Jewish and black communities, were at a boiling point. Predators and crazies seemed to rule the streets. Aggressive panhandlers were everywhere. So-called "Squeegee Kids" descended on cars at busy intersections, ran a dirty sponge over windshields and demanded money for this "service." Drunks and junkies urinated on the sidewalks, seemingly without consequence.

It was so bad the *New York Post* tabloid ran a front page headline in huge type imploring the mayor: 'DAVE, DO SOMETHING." And Time magazine piled on in superb fashion, running a cover story a few months later entitled: "The Rotting of the Big Apple."

In 1993, new mayor Rudolph W. Guiliani was swept into office on the promise of change. A former hard-nosed federal prosecutor, Guiliani vowed to get tough on crime and quickly hired a career law enforcement heavyweight named Bill Bratton as his new police commissioner.

Bratton, who had headed the New York City Transit Police and the Boston Police Department before taking over the NYPD, was very popular with the rank and file. Bratton "got" what policing was all about. And he knew how to motivate people.

In his earlier stint with the transit cops, he had ditched their bland light blue uniform shirts and outfitted them with sharp-looking dark shirts and commando sweaters. He'd also replaced their old side-arms with 9 mm revolvers, a significant upgrade in firepower. The troops loved their new look – it put some swagger in their step.

Meanwhile, those of us in the regular PD were envious. We were still wearing old-fashioned uniforms with light blue shirts that screamed: condo maintenance man. We looked like we were there to fix your air-conditioner.

Now, as commissioner of the NYPD, Bratton began energetically assembling his new team. John Miller, a high-profile TV newsman whom I'd known for years, became Bratton's deputy commissioner of public information. And Jack Maple, who would become a great friend and like a brother to me, was named deputy commissioner of crime control strategies.

Maple and I had actually met way back in 1981, when I was a patrolman in Manhattan and ran down to a subway platform to break up a fight. One of the combatants, it turned out, was Maple, who was on plainclothes duty as a transit cop and trying to make an arrest.

He had a big, bushy beard back then and was wearing a Playboy sweater and pink Converse sneakers. I mistook him for the bad guy – or a weirdly-dressed skell at the very least. In fact, I was just about to crack him over the head with my nightstick when he looked up and shouted "No, I'm on the job!" Meaning he was a cop, too.

As the commander of DOI now, I was one of the promising young lieutenants in the NYPD, and Bratton's new team soon reached out to me.

First, Miller called me to a clandestine meeting in the back of a black car. He was gathering intelligence on the commissioner's new command staff and produced a book with the profiles of every chief in the NYPD, asking my opinion of each.

A short while later, at a black-tie New Year's Eve party at Miller's apartment, I renewed my acquaintance with Maple and congratulated him on his new position. And within weeks, I was working for him as the commander of the police commissioner's investigative unit, charged with looking into all types of extremely sensitive cases that concerned the new boss.

Some of these were Internal Affairs cases: in one, we looked into a captain rumored to be spending his working days with his girlfriend at her apartment. Others were potentially more deadly, such as the time the picture of an informant of ours somehow ended up on the front page of *The New York Times*.

After a panicked call from a superior, a detective named Jimmy Nuciforo and I made a hurried trip to Harlem, found the informant on a street corner, threw him in the car and took him to a hotel for his own protection.

Working for Jack Maple was an experience unlike any other.

The man was the proverbial "piece of work." He was the quintessential New Yorker, a tough-talking Queens guy who rose through the ranks as a street cop. Whip-smart and a savant on all matters of crime and policing, he was funny, ribald, exacting – and a ton of fun to be around.

Oh, there were times I wanted to poke his eyes out with pencils, because he tested you constantly. But he made you work harder in shitty conditions than you ever thought you could.

His wardrobe had certainly changed over the years, too, which was a source of tremendous amusement to the rest of the department. A short, stout man – his nickname was "Fatso" – he now dressed like a dandy, favoring finely-tailored suits, bow ties, Homburg hats and spectator shoes, polished to a high gloss.

But even if he looked like a character straight out of "Guys and Dolls," Jack Maple was determined to shake up the NYPD.

In his estimation, it had grown stagnant and woefully inadequate at fulfilling its central mission, which was to fight crime and catch crooks.

To operate effectively, he felt, every police department needed to concentrate on four principals:

1. Accurate timely intelligence.
2. Rapid deployment.
3. Effective tactics.
4. Relentless follow-up and assessment.

So he mapped out each precinct and pinpointed where crimes had occurred, giving each precinct commander a better overall picture of what the crime situation was in his district. Incredibly, this was the first time in NYPD history that patterns of crime were being tracked in real time. Maple also instituted weekly meetings at which he and the department's top brass grilled these commanders – and not gently – on what the hell they were doing to bring crime down.

The meetings were called Comstat, named for the ancient computer used to collate and store crime statistics back then.

Another of his first moves was to make me the head of a unit charged with tracking down fugitives, then a huge problem for the NYPD.

As Maple would write of that time in his book, "The Crime Fighter": "In the previous two years alone, at least 12,000 people who had been positively identified as the perpetrators of violent crimes in New York City hadn't been arrested for those crimes.

"These crimes weren't page one material, so the suspects, instead of being hunted down and thrown in the pokey, had suffered no further inconvenience than that their names were entered into index cards and filed in drawers marked WANTED."

Nothing fried Maple more than to ask a commander about someone who was wanted for murder, or for a series of violent robberies, and be told: "We can't find the guy. He's in the wind, commissioner."

So Maple sent me, Nuciforo, a terrific detective named Sonny Archer and a few others to Brooklyn's dangerous 75th Precinct, where some 300 bad guys were wanted for violent crimes.

"Don't show your faces again," he told us, "until you catch 100 people."

Our mission, in effect, was to quickly round up as many of the fugitives as we could so Jack could embarrass the lazy commanders who'd thrown up their hands at the problem.

I wanted to embarrass them, too.

"Look, these bad guys didn't go to South America for plastic surgery," I'd tell my men. "They're not Carlos the Jackal. They're around here somewhere. And we'll get them."

Every morning at 4:30, we'd literally get dressed in the darkened streets. We'd pull up in a van and put on our black pants, black bullet-proof vests and black gun-belts. It was a serious ninja look. Well, only if ninjas wore baseball caps.

Sonny Archer would then produce a package of manila envelopes crammed with info – including photos and last known addresses – of a dozen wanted suspects. Then we'd hit a neighborhood or two and go look for them.

There was a whole art to finding people who were wanted. Sonny was a terrific tracker and we used some creative methods to ferret out these fugitives. We had a ton of disguises and posed as UPS delivery men, Job Corps workers, housing project maintenance men, anything that allowed us to get close to the criminals we were looking for.

On one occasion, when we were having a particularly hard time tracking a man wanted for murder, Sonny somehow got the name of the man's girlfriend and her work phone number. Once we found out where she worked, we had one our detectives, posing as a delivery man for a local florist, surprise her with a dozen roses.

A card attached to the roses said they were from "Anonymous." She immediately thought they were from her boyfriend. We waited for her to get off work and followed her home. And we quickly confirmed that her boyfriend lived at the same address, which just as quickly led to his arrest.

We arrested another fugitive, wanted for multiple murders, when he showed up for his mother's funeral. Hey, even crooks turn out for family events. So we had undercover detectives sprinkled throughout the funeral home, signing the visitors' book and chatting with the other mourners until the murderer appeared and was arrested.

We even managed to apprehend a fugitive by literally annoying him into handcuffs.

This was a dangerous stick-up guy named McBee, believed to be armed with a Mac-10 assault pistol. Once we discovered where he lived, we showed up at his apartment door one day at the crack of dawn.

First we listened for noise. Sure enough, we could hear kids' voices and the sound of a TV, as well as the occasional voices of a man and woman. But when we knocked, no one answered. Instead, the apartment suddenly grew quiet.

We didn't have a court warrant for this guy, just a "want" card. That meant he'd been identified as a suspect in a crime and was wanted. Technically, then, we couldn't arrest him until he stepped out of the apartment. And he apparently wasn't coming out voluntarily.

To "persuade" him to come out, we launched into our own little version of a psy-ops campaign, with the intention of getting on the guy's nerves.

Remember the classic tactic the FBI used on the Branch Davidians during the Waco siege in Texas in the early 1990's? How they blasted loud, annoying music (Nancy Sinatra's "These Boots Are Made for Walking" was a favorite) and sounds of sheep being slaughtered to coerce David Koresh and his loony followers into giving up?

Looking back on it now, I think what we did next to McBee was even worse.

Sonny Archer kept knocking.

I took a quarter out of my pocket and starting tapping on the door.

And Jimmy Nuciforo added a different percussion to the mix, rapping on the door with his detective's ring.

Soon we added a new and even more obnoxious element: singing. And not *good* singing, either.

"MC-BEE!" we cried in an other-worldly falsetto. "MC-BEEEEE! MC-BEEEEEE!"

After a few hours, the girlfriend cracked. Wordlessly, she left the apartment with the children.

Still, we kept it up: the knocking, the rapping, the tapping, the shrill crooning of "MC-BEEE!" that echoed off the apartment's steel door and down the hallway.

It took another hour, but finally the door opened and thoroughly worn-looking McBee gave himself up.

All our hard work in this new job, all our persistence, began paying dividends from the very beginning.

By the end of the first week chasing fugitives, Sonny, Jimmy and I had already managed to arrest 14 of them. Maple was thrilled. Soon he would have us chasing missing bad guys in other parts of the city, too.

"Gee," he needled chief of detectives Joe Borelli, according to "The Crime Fighter," "my Naugahyde squad caught 14 crooks in a week working out of their cars in the Seven-Five. Imagine if we had sent some real cops to do the job."

This he would punctuate with a loud cackle. Hey, if the boss was happy, I was happy. And the boss was practically blissed-out.

I was working 12- and 14-hour days, getting no sleep, existing on coffee and adrenaline. But I felt good. I knew we were doing important work. I knew that my mentor, Jack Maple, was changing the very culture of the NYPD, bringing effective new methods, computerization and accountability to crime-fighting that was making the city safer.

And I had a front-row seat to watch the whole glorious mission unfold.

6

The Cold Case Squad

As hectic as the job was by the fall of 1994, there was also a familiar rhythm to it that was comforting.

In the morning, I'd be out with my little faux-Ninja squad, doing investigations, tracking fugitives and locking them up. In the afternoon, I'd put on a suit, go down to headquarters and handle administrative duties for the rest of the day.

But that all changed in October with my promotion to captain, a move that would turbo-charge my ascent up the ranks.

In order to become a captain, a candidate had to pass the Civil Service exam. But once you hit captain, the sky was the limit for your career. Every rank attained after that was a discretionary appointment made at the pleasure of the police commissioner. And there were many higher ranks that an ambitious and hard-working young captain could aspire to.

Still, now that I was a captain, it was hard to justify my continuing in my present role. Captains commanded precincts. They commanded 200 to 400 people, uniform and civilian, and generally had enormous responsibility. So because I had shown I was good at investigations and fugitive hunting, the logical landing place for me was the Warrant Division.

This was a big squad. There were some 500 investigators in the Warrant Division, which investigated old arrest warrants that precinct detectives hadn't cleared. There was one central office in Manhattan and satellite offices in each borough.

But when I sat down with one of my lieutenants, Vertel Martin, to examine how the division worked, I was appalled.

For one thing, we discovered the Warrant Division was basically working Monday to Friday, 9 a.m. – 5 p.m. This is a wonderful schedule if you work in a bank or run a souvenir shop in a sleepy seaside village. But not if your job is catching crooks in the big city.

You didn't have to be Columbo to figure out that the bad guys probably wouldn't be home if you were calling on them at, say, noon. If they weren't out robbing or assaulting someone, they were probably having a nice quiet lunch somewhere.

But getting the division to accept new ways of doing things wasn't easy.

It's hard to tell people: "For X amount of years, you've been working Monday to Friday with weekends off, getting home at 7 in the evening like a regular person. Well, now you're gonna wake up at 3 in the morning. And we're gonna hit our first door by 5 a.m. at the latest."

Oh, God, some of my men wanted to burn my house down when they heard about their new schedules! They *hated* me!

But we had a lot of success from the outset. We went from catching 6,000 fugitives a year to catching 12,000 and getting all this attention and publicity from the media.

And all those grumpy lieutenants who were really unhappy with me when I took over? Now they were thrilled! Because now they were piling up tons of overtime and making money. Now we were considered an elite unit, a place where other cops desperately wanted to work.

The culture had changed so much that at the end of that first year, for Christmas, all the lieutenants chipped in and bought me this beautiful – and expensive – humidor for my cigars.

"Captain," one said when they presented me with the gift, "when you got here, we wanted to slash your tires. But you got us from fishing for crappies in the Chattahoochee River to fishing for marlin. Thank you."

Bill Bratton, the new commissioner, was understandably delighted with the results the squad was getting, too. And he was delighted with all the national attention, too.

He wanted to make a statement that this was a new day for the NYPD, and that all the old, ineffective ways of doing business were being thrown out the window. So he selected a few standout captains throughout the department, most of them young, for promotion.

No longer would promotions go to the guy with the grayest hair, as they had for decades. Before, the thinking among the rank-and-file was: *Whether I bust my ass or not, the reward is the same.*

But now Bratton was signaling that promotion-by-geriatrics was a thing of the past. *If you perform*, he was saying, *I don't care how old you are. You can be rewarded here.*

This proved to be a brilliant motivational move. And so it was that 11 months after attaining the rank of captain, I was promoted to Deputy Inspector at the age of 35.

I was assigned to the detective bureau in Queens South as the deputy inspector in charge of all detectives, where I languished for a while pushing papers and doing administrative stuff. It was boring and frustrating. Every time I tried to go out in the field and pull homicides, I was told to come back to the office.

Finally I went to Jack Maple with a simple plea.

"Give me *something*," I asked. "Give me a precinct *somewhere*. Let me get back to police work. I'm totally wasting my abilities."

Jack could hear the urgency in my voice.

"OK," he said, "what could you do?"

"What if we had a unit," I proposed, "to investigate old murders?"

The fact was, there were so many murders in New York at the time that the police were simply overwhelmed.

Detectives were assigned to investigate murders on a rotating catch system. It worked like this: Detective Jones catches one, two days later Detective Smith catches one, then Detective Adams catches one. And then we're back to Detective Jones, because it's a week or two later, and now he's got another homicide. Except he still hasn't solved the first one.

But now he has a fresh homicide and maybe it's a bigger news story. Maybe it's high-profile because the tabloids are heating it up pretty good, putting pressure on the brass to get this thing solved. So now Detective Jones puts the first homicide to the side and starts working on the second one, and then he catches a third one and . . . well, you get the picture.

So it goes on and on like this. And somehow the first murder ends up in a drawer, with very little attention paid to it. And then Detective Jones gets promoted to sergeant, he goes somewhere else, and no one ever looks at that old homicide.

Now multiply that across a huge department, where thousands of murders are piling up. At the time, New York had an average of 1,500-2,000 murders every year. If even 200 murder cases a year are shunted to the side, in five years you have 1,000 murders that have not been worked on – and therefore not solved. And that was probably a conservative figure.

So I proposed to Jack: "How about I start working on those old murders?' And he liked the idea."

So we started pulling cases. And I started working with Louie Anemone, who was now the chief of the department, selling him and Jack on how much our work would benefit the city.

My premise was: people don't commit a murder and go drive a truck or work a straight job after that. They're in the drug business, or they're enforcers, or they're just general criminal scumbags. And they're going to continue to commit crimes until you stop them.

So if they've committed a murder, chances are they're still robbing people, or shooting people, or doing other terrible things. So if we started to catch these guys, crime would definitely go down.

That was the real selling point for Jack and Louie – aside from the obvious, that any murderer should be caught.

Jack asked me how a unit looking into old murders would be structured. I told him I'd have a mix of homicide investigators and fugitive detectives, because half of a murder investigation is finding the suspect.

Maple, bless his heart, agreed to my plan.

I was quietly yanked out of the Queens South detective bureau and given my pick of whoever I wanted to make up this new unit. I quickly chose Sonny Archer and Jimmy Nuciforo among a select – and diverse – group that had worked with me in narcotics.

"Not every detective is a superstar," I told author Stacy Horn for her 2005 book "The Restless Sleep: Inside New York City's Cold Case Squad." "It's true in every business or corporation; it's the same at IBM or Mrs. Field's Cookies, and the police department is no different.

"In the Detective Squad you've got one or two guys who are real warriors, one or two lunkheads who shouldn't be there, and the rest are guys who do what they're told to do. You assign them a case and they'll do a decent job. But that's *all* they're going to do for you. They're not going to knock themselves out."

Of course, we wanted the warriors. I went out and got as many as I could. And this, then, was the beginning of the NYPD's first Cold Case and Apprehension Squad.

We were not exactly given palatial digs for the monumental task that lay before us.

Bratton and Maple did not want it to look as if my squad and I were getting special privileges. So we had to find out own office to work out of. We found a place in Brooklyn that looked more like a storage room, filled with dust, cobwebs and broken furniture.

We had to clean it up ourselves, furnish it ourselves, have desks delivered and phones installed.

Then we went to work. We started pulling cases. And of course, the resistance we got right off the bat from other chiefs and detectives was ridiculous.

The chief of detectives, a tall, silver-haired 39-year veteran named Charles Reuther, wanted there to be special criteria for which cases we could investigate. Like you could only take a case if the detective who had worked on it was retired or dead.

No one wanted to be embarrassed for doing – or condoning – sloppy work in the past.

"They're going to go in and try to find something we didn't do," one anonymous detective fumed about us to the *Daily News*.

Being allowed to look only into certain cases frustrated all of us. But when the unit was moved under the authority of Lou Anemone instead of Reuther, that problem disappeared.

Eddie Norris, Anemone told the *Daily News*, would have "the authority of the chief of department to go in and pull cases rather than running into problems in the detective bureau, creating a lot of animosity."

Freed of the constraints created by inter-departmental bickering, the Cold Case Squad started kicking ass.

Within six weeks, we solved 27 murders. It was a stunning number. And these weren't what were called "fake arrests," where the murderer was already in prison, or dead, and you had simply figured out who he was.

No, these were guys put in handcuffs for the first time for the crime they had committed. These were "real" arrests for "real" open murder cases. Our success attracted quite a bit of media attention, first in New York and then nationally when NPR's Melissa Block featured the Cold Case squad on her "All Things Considered" show.

Though it all, there was tremendous pressure on me. The top brass had given me this squad, and they continued to want results.

So I pushed my guys hard. I pushed them *really* hard. I think I'm a decent guy. But I can be a bit of an asshole. I'm aware of that. I'd push my guys to the point of embarrassing them. After all, the whole reason we were there was because there had undoubtedly been some sloppy or lazy detective work done in the past. And I didn't want my guys to be that way.

I definitely didn't want them just hanging around the office killing time. They were supposed to be out looking for criminals. So if I saw someone reading, say, the *Daily News* sports pages at his desk, I'd start reading over his shoulder.

"Oh, is that him?" I'd ask innocently.

"What do you mean?" the detective would say, looking up.

"Is that the suspect there?" I'd say, pointing to a photo. "God, it looks like he's wearing a Yankees' uniform! Who the fuck is that? Are we looking for him? Now get the fuck out of here! Go catch somebody!"

Jonathan Cumbo, I remember, was a good detective going through a particularly long dry spell of solving cases. He was also a friend of mine of many years. Which of course made him a prime target for the Deputy Inspector to torture unmercifully.

"Jonathan," I'd say loudly, in front of the others, "let me ask you this: are you ever gonna catch anybody again? I just want to know. I'm not mad at you. I just need to know. 'Cause if you're not gonna catch anybody . . ."

He got the message. He was a good cop and a good human being. But that's how I would push my guys every day. I was already unpopular – people in the office were circulating 8x10 photo-shopped images of me with horns coming out of my head. And now I was making the problem worse.

Within months, as we became more and more successful – and more and more well-known – the general public began calling and writing for our help.

Some of the entreaties were heart-wrenching. This one's son was killed – could we look into the case? This one's mother had been murdered – no leads, please help. We began investigating other violent crimes, such as rapes, as well.

Now we had officially become known, in a strange parlance of cop lingo and FM radio jargon, as "that squad that does requests."

During it all, my career was rocketing on an upper trajectory I could never have envisioned.

As far as my bosses were concerned, I was the Golden Boy, destined for greater and greater things. A woman from RKO, the film production and distribution company, called to say they were interested in doing a TV series on the squad.

"Would you consider being a consultant for the show?" she asked. "With a contract that would pay, oh, $40,000 the first year?"

"Uh, yeah," I answered, my eyes practically bulging out of my head, "I think that might work."

It sounded like a pretty great part-time job. And it wasn't exactly like wielding a pick in a coal mine.

Rubbing elbows with TV stars, grazing at the catered on-set buffet, occasionally waving dismissively at an actor and sniffing: "No, that's *not* how you pull a gun out of a holster!" – how hard could it be?

Yes, life was setting up particularly well for young Deputy Inspector Eddie Norris.

Then, without any warning, it all began to crater.

7

Dead Man Walking

In the spring of 1996, a reordering of the NYPD hierarchy occurred with all the subtlety of a Third World palace coup.

My buddy, John Miller, had been the first to go, fired earlier as deputy commissioner of public information. He was crushed, the move seeming all the more ominous because he was never really told why he was terminated.

Then a few months after we got the Cold Case squad up and running, Bill Bratton, who had famously vowed to "take the city back block by block," resigned as police commissioner after only 27 months on the job.

It was generally agreed that Bratton had been pushed out by mayor Rudy Giuliani. There was no shortage of theories as to why. The most popular held that Giuliani resented all the attention Bratton was getting for lowering the city's crime rate.

Just two months earlier, Bratton had appeared on the cover of *Time* magazine, under the headline: "Finally, We're Winning the War Against Crime. Here's Why." The good mayor's photo, on the other hand, was nowhere to be found.

There was also talk that Giuliani felt Bratton was moving too fast in his quest to modernize and reform the NYPD. Whatever the reason, Jack Maple, my mentor and protector, loyally followed Bratton out the door.

Uh-oh, I thought when I heard Maple was leaving. *I'm doomed. This is not good at all.*

All of a sudden, I had no political protection at all in the department. And nobody needed protection more than I did.

The fact was that all these plum assignments I'd received – working in the commissioner's office, working for Jack Maple, heading up the Warrant Division and the Cold Case Squad – had created a lot of embarrassment for a lot of people.

I had made a ton of enemies. So many people in the department were convinced my goal in life was to make them look bad – and nothing could have been further from the truth.

We weren't trying to embarrass people. We were trying to solve crimes. We were trying to lock up bad guys, plain and simple.

And yet this hyper-sensitivity to being embarrassed pisses me off to this day, because it's so pervasive in policing in America.

Let me get this straight: we would rather let a murderer go free than have somebody in the department be embarrassed? Really? How does that even register with people? Because I can't justify that in my own mind.

OK, Detective Jones in the 44th Precinct may look bad on one particular case. First of all, who's going to know? So he didn't catch the bad guy for whatever reason. Maybe he was over-worked. Maybe he was incompetent, maybe he wasn't. Maybe he was a great detective with too much on his plate.

What's the difference? Isn't the goal to catch bad people?

But that was definitely the message that was tacitly conveyed throughout the department, especially when I ran the Cold Case Squad: don't fucking embarrass anyone.

Nobody wanted to rock the boat. And I never abided by that philosophy – ever.

So now, with Bratton and Maple gone, I became a pariah.

"They're gonna come kill me next," I told my inner circle on the Cold Case Squad. "That black Cadillac is gonna pull up and I'm gonna get that ride. But you guys should go. Pick a place in the department where you want to go. I'll try to help you get there."

Most of the guys, however, remained intensely loyal to me.

"No, I came with you and I'll go with you anywhere," said detective Rick Burnham, a sentiment expressed by others. "I don't care if it's foot patrol in the Bronx."

My enemies, though, were cackling gleefully at the thought of me twisting in the wind. They were sure I was about to get my comeuppance.

During a routine visit to the 13th floor of police headquarters not long after Maple announced he was leaving, I ran into chief of detectives Charlie Reuther.

"Ha! Dead Man Walking" he chortled. Which was exactly how I felt at that point.

Reuther wasn't the only one writing me off. Even before Bratton and Maple were gone, other chiefs had told me directly: "Eddie, your career's over when they leave. You know that, right?"

So now, with Maple gone, I was basically radioactive. No one wanted to be seen with me. Or heard talking to me. Or linked to me in any way.

It was during this time that Mayor Giuliani appointed Howard Safir as the new police commissioner. All I knew about Safir is that he had been the Fire Commissioner of New York before taking over the top job with the police, and that he'd done some kind of comedy bit on David Letterman's show.

But Safir, a tall man with baleful eyes and a formidable presence, turned out to have an extensive background in law enforcement. Before taking the top job with the Fire Department, he'd had a stellar career with the DEA and the U.S. Marshall's Service, where he was Chief of the Witness Security Division.

Soon, he would also prove to be one of my biggest benefactors.

On May 11, 1996, I married the love of my life, Kathryn. She worked at Faconnable, a high-end French clothing store, where I'd met her while shopping for shirts for Jack Maple. (Maple at the time was like a nutty professor-type. He was divorced and too busy for mundane stuff like clothes-shopping. So he'd give me wads of cash and send me off with gruff instructions to take care of it for him.)

When Kathryn and I returned from our honeymoon in Bermuda, a couple of my detectives picked us up at the airport. They arrived bearing news.

"The commissioner wants to see you in his office," one told me.

"Oh, yeah?" I said. "What's this about?"

"It's about you," was the answer.

My heart sank. Even in the best of times, you never wanted to hear that you were the subject of a sit-down with the commissioner. And these were hardly the best of times, not with so many of the department higher-ups licking their chops and thinking: *Payback time for Eddie Norris! Can't wait to see it!*

As it happened, Safir had also requested the presence at this meeting of the chiefs of detectives from the various boroughs. Lou Anemone was there, too. But he was the only friend in a roomful of hostile faces glowering at me when I sat down.

Quickly, it became apparent that the meeting was about the Cold Case Squad and my role in heading it. And just as quickly, it became evident that, aside from Louie, the other chiefs wanted it disbanded.

Safir asked me why I formed the squad, and I told him. But Reuther attacked me immediately. He basically called me a fraud and said the Cold Case Squad was stealing cases and doing a horseshit job all around.

All the other chiefs, except Louie, soon happily joined in ripping me.

"He's embarrassing us," one said.

"He's taking easy cases," said another.

He's doing this, he's doing that – the accusations flew one after another. None of them were true.

But the long knives were out, and I felt cornered. Then an eerie sort of calm settled over me.

They're going to kill me anyway, I thought, *so fuck it. I'm going to speak plainly and defend myself.*

Now things got even more heated.

I began quizzing the other chiefs, asking them what they knew of how we worked, insisting that the success of our squad was based on sound detective work, perseverance and the ability to spend more time with the cases – not on any special privileges or crime-fighting tools unavailable to the rest of the department.

"We use the same computers you use," I said. "Like the CARS computer that every squad has."

All around the room, there were puzzled expressions.

"What the fuck is the CARS computer?" one chief demanded.

I explained the acronym stood for Computer Assisted Robbery System, which basically compiled lists of criminal suspects for investigation.

"You're a chief of detectives and you don't know what the CARS computer is?" I asked, zeroing in on the poor dunce. "Shouldn't *you* be the one who's embarrassed, and not me?"

I mentioned a couple of other acronyms and the chiefs looked at me as if I were speaking Mandarin Chinese.

But I was on dangerous ground here. I was arguing with men who out-ranked me by five levels. Anemone was the only one defending me.

Suddenly, some 15 minutes into the meeting, Safir raised one of his huge hands – believe me, you would not want this guy giving you a prostate exam – and slammed it on his desk.

"I got it," he said firmly. "I understand the issue."

And he walked out of the room. End of meeting.

When Anemone and I got on the elevator to leave, I said: "Dude, I'm dead. Just do me a favor and put me in a precinct somewhere. I'll go anywhere. I'll go back to a uniform. Just get me away from these guys. They're gonna make my life miserable."

"All right," Louie said. "We'll figure something out."

A week later, though, I was summoned before the commissioner once more. I was in my dress blues and clearly nervous when I was ushered into his office. But Safir put me at ease right away.

"Eddie," he said, "tell me what's wrong with the department."

Huh?

Yet this time I was hesitant about telling the truth. I was already in enough trouble. Ripping the department didn't strike me as a wise move. *Instead of being yourself*, I thought, *be smart. Try NOT to be yourself for once.*

"Sir," I answered, "this is a great agency. I don't know what we could do to improve it. We have a lot of smart people here."

Safir shot me a withering look.

"Cut the bullshit," he growled. "Don't waste my time. What's wrong with this place?"

"You really want to know?" I said.

Apparently, he did. So for the next 30 minutes, virtually without a break, I ticked off all the things that pissed me off about the department: people not working the proper hours, people being lazy, people being rewarded who should never be rewarded, the twisted idea that it was better for a murderer to go free than to embarrass a detective who didn't do his job, etc.

On and on I went. Safir listened intently until I was through.

"OK," he said finally, "how would you fix things?"

I told him all the things I would do.

"The key to reducing crime is not a uniform presence," I told him. "The key to reducing crime is investigation. You go out and you drag these motherfuckers from their beds at 4 in the morning and put them in handcuffs. You do it in big numbers and crime goes down. It's not rocket science. It's fairly simple. But we're not doing that.

"Say you've got a guy who's doing burglaries or robberies or whatever," I continued. "He does so many in a week. Pick a number. Pick 10. If you get him today as opposed to six months from now – or,

God forbid, *never* – you've prevented all those crimes from occurring in the future. Do that in big enough numbers, think about how many people you've saved in the city."

The commissioner ended the meeting shortly after. Soon I began to hear from Louie Anemone and others that Safir had something in mind for me.

Hmmm, I thought, *maybe I'll get a nice job somewhere after all. Maybe I'm even on the road to inspector at age 36!*

Ten days later, Safir again summoned me to a meeting. As was his style, he got right to the point.

"I want you to be deputy commissioner of operations," he said.

I was floored. Was he serious? He was offering me Jack Maple's old job?

"I . . . I'm not Jack Maple," I managed to stammer.

Are you crazy? I wanted to scream. *You're asking me to replace one of my best friends, the guy who's helped revolutionize law enforcement agencies all over the world with his Comstat system and his bold new ideas! It's like you're asking me to step in after Muhammad Ali or something!*

"I don't want you to be Jack Maple," Safir said. "I want you to be Eddie Norris. That's all I want. I want you to walk around here and . . . no, I want you to STOMP around here! You walk in this office without knocking anytime you want.

"I want people to know you're my guy, and you can look at anything you want, any aspect of the department. You have complete authority. *My* authority."

I was almost too stunned to talk.

Two weeks earlier, my career had been on life support. No Bratton or Jack Maple around, no one to watch my back, the rest of the chiefs ready to whack me the minute they could.

And now this was happening. Whatever *this* was.

It was one of the most surreal moments of my life. I don't think I ever actually said I would take the job. Again, the police department is a paramilitary organization. You don't ask. You just do.

The fact was, I had a new job – whether I liked it or not.

"Who . . . who do I report to?" I said at last.

On his desk, Safir had the NYPD organizational chart that represented over 50,000 employees – four times more than the FBI – operating on a budget of over $2 billion. He pointed to the top of the chart.

"Here's me," he said. He pointed to a space directly below. "And here's you."

Next he drew a straight line from Commissioner to Deputy Commissioner of Operations. I was right at the top of the hierarchy. The only people higher than me were the Chief of the Department and the First Deputy Commissioner.

What happened next was almost equally unreal.

Safir stepped away from his desk, an ornate 122-year-old piece of furniture once used by Teddy Roosevelt. (Roosevelt had been the president of the board of the New York Police Commissioners before becoming the country's 26th president.) The two of us walked out of his beautiful office and across the carpeted floor to his conference room, with its stunning view of Manhattan.

Waiting for us there was the command staff of the department. There were some 20 people in the room: eight deputy commissioners including the ones in charge of public information, community affairs and budget, plus all these bureau chiefs, including some of the ones who hated me.

Everyone was staring at me. I had presented reports in front of many of them in the past. Now, I guess they thought I was about to give another report – maybe on fugitive hunting or something – that they would immediately deem more bullshit.

Instead, Safir cleared his throat.

"I guess you're all wondering why Eddie's here," he began. "I just named him commissioner of operations. I want him to look at all your shops. He has complete authority. He speaks for me and begins immediately."

With that, Safir banged one of his meaty paws on the table, turned to the First Deputy Commissioner and said: "OK, what do you have for me?"

And that was it.

Now it was on to the business of the day.

I was still astonished. Lou Anemone pulled up a chair for me. I sat and looked around at the equally-dumbfounded faces staring back at me, including Charlie Reuther's.

You could read the panic sweeping through the room: *Holy shit! This is the guy we were threatening! And now we work for him!*

In her book "The Restless Sleep," author Stacy Horn labeled that moment "Dead Chiefs Sitting." And that was about right. Reuther was soon ousted as chief of detectives and took a job heading up the less prestigious Criminal Justice Bureau. Others would soon follow him out the door, grumbling about their mistreatment and no doubt cursing me along the way.

Meanwhile, the Cold Case Squad would thrive now that their old boss, former Dead Man Walking Eddie Norris, was the new Deputy Commissioner of Operations. Whatever manpower they needed, whatever equipment they needed, whatever bureaucratic bullshit they needed to quietly disappear, it was theirs in the blink of an eye.

(The squad would get even more publicity when the CBS TV series "Cold Case" debuted in 2003, even though it was about a fictionalized unit in the Philadelphia Police Department. My new promotion, though, now precluded me from having any role with the show.)

As for me, I essentially took over Jack Maple's role. I was now in charge of creating and implementing crime-fighting strategies for the department. I worked in Jack's old office, sat in his chair, took over his staff.

Now it was me briefing Mayor Rudy Giuliani every Thursday and coming to him with suggestions on how to better the department and make it more efficient. At one point, I put together a big proposal asking him to hire 1,373 new officers that were desperately needed in some of the city's worst neighborhoods.

All the older guys in the office made fun of me.

"Ha, you're gonna ask the mayor for 1,300 new cops?" they'd say. "Good luck with that one. He's gonna fucking *scream* at you."

But when I made my big, formal presentation to the mayor at City Hall, with Howard Safir looking on and beaming like a proud uncle, Giuliani was silent for a moment, his face impassive.

"Tell you what," he said at last. "Let's make it an even 1,500 new cops."

Score one for the new guy. I don't think I stopped smiling all day.

Another part of my duties was to run Jack's beloved Comstat meetings twice a week. These were often tense three-hour sessions in which the command staff and uniform guys with the rank of captain or above were grilled about crime in their precincts and their methods for attacking it.

My staff and I prepped for these meetings for hours. We looked at major crime patterns all over the city, what strategies were working, which ones weren't, and where the ball was being dropped in certain cases.

There is no other way to say it: the weak-link commanders were thoroughly beaten up in these meetings.

Some would lose their jobs if they consistently under-performed. But my feeling was: if you had a store that was constantly losing money, how long would you keep the store manager? Eventually, you'd have to make a change, wouldn't you?

The same principal applied with the NYPD. Only here it was critically *more* important to have strong leaders, because people's lives were at stake. And for too long, weak commanders who wouldn't make changes had been countenanced in the NYPD. Often this was because they had been on the job for ages. But often it was also because no one wanted to – here comes that word again – *embarrass* anyone.

In any event, all our hard work in the next few years started to pay dividends.

The crime rate in New York went down, and all the attendant media attention led to requests for me to lecture at police departments all over the U.S., and in France and Germany as well.

Life was good for Eddie Norris again. I was working my tail off, but having fun, too. The city was a safer place, my bosses loved me and in June of 1999, I became a new dad when my son, Jack, was born.

Then one day in November, the phone rang in my Manhattan apartment.

The mayor-elect of Baltimore was on the line.

And he wasn't calling to chat about the weather.

8

Welcome to Charm City

It's safe to say that our conversation did not get off to a rousing start.

"I'm Martin O'Malley and I'm going to be the mayor of Baltimore," the voice on the other end said. "I'd like to talk to you about a job."

I replied in my usual gentle, understated way.

"Who the fuck *is* this?" I said. "I don't have time for this shit."

Was somebody from my office pranking me? God knows those assholes were capable of it.

"No, really, I *am* O'Malley," the voice said. "I just won the election."

As I would soon learn, both statements were true. The voters of Baltimore had just elected as their leader the young, charismatic former prosecutor who wore muscle T-shirts, played guitar and fronted an Irish rock band.

In a majority black city, Martin O'Malley, a white city councilman, had pulled off an improbable victory, soundly defeating two African-American opponents by vowing to reduce Baltimore's staggering levels of crime with what was being labeled a "zero tolerance" form of policing.

(Also called the "broken windows" approach, it basically involved cracking down on minor offenses in the hope that would also lead to a reduction of major crimes, something we'd done, in one way or another, in New York for years.)

Dimly, I recalled that O'Malley had been part of a fact-finding delegation that had visited NYPD headquarter years earlier, looking for ways to make Baltimore safer. He and the others had even sat in on our Comstat meetings. And they had come away impressed with how our policing methods and computerized, performance-based system had dramatically lowered violent crime levels in the largest city in America.

Apparently, Baltimore's mayor-elect had also reached out to Jack Maple for advice on filling the top law enforcement slots in his new administration. Since leaving the NYPD, Maple was doing consulting work for big-city police departments with his partner, John Linder. And both men had recommended me highly.

Now, O'Malley was asking me to come down to Baltimore to meet him and see if I would be a good fit in his new administration.

The truth was, I was immediately intrigued.

For one thing, it was my 20th year on the job with the NYPD, which meant I could soon retire, collect my full pension and start a new career. I was still young, only 39. And as the Deputy Commissioner of Operations, with a big role in New York's extraordinary crime turn-around, I knew it was just a matter of time before a slew of job offers started rolling in.

There were also other quality-of-life issues to consider.

Manhattan was an incredibly expensive place to live. My son, Jack, was an infant and both my wife and I were working. Together, we were making decent money. But this being New York, we were basically just getting by.

I'm a native New Yorker, but it's a tough place to live unless you're very wealthy. If you're making seven figures, sure, you can have a nice town house and send the kids to private school and have a comfortable life. Otherwise, good luck affording all the charms the city has to offer.

Finally, there was this: I missed being in uniform. I missed running the streets and locking up bad guys. Maybe I'd be able to do some of that again in Baltimore. It was definitely worth exploring.

The following Monday, I went to see Howard Safir and told him all about O'Malley's job offer – even though nothing concrete had been discussed.

"You deserve it," the commissioner said. "I'm happy for you."

Yet he also had a concerned look on his face.

"You know," he said after a pause, "Baltimore's a very dangerous place."

"Commissioner," I said, "I did the most dangerous work we have here, which was chasing down fugitives for years. I was in the projects every morning of my career, it seemed."

Safir shook his head.

"I don't mean *that* kind of dangerous," he said. "I mean politically dangerous. Just be careful."

At the time, I didn't really know what he meant. Now I do. Safir had always been a savvy guy. And his conversations with Baltimore's previous police commissioner, Thomas Frazier, had convinced him that there was a poisonous racial dynamic at play within the police department, the City Council and ordinary citizens that could made policing in Baltimore exceedingly difficult.

But I was blithely ignorant of all that when I took the train to Baltimore two days later and met O'Malley in the bar at the Hyatt Regency Inner Harbor.

He was accompanied by Michael Enright, who would become the city's First Deputy Mayor. O'Malley was charming as could be. He told me how impressed he was with what I had done in New York. And he picked my brain about various crime-fighting strategies, wanting to know if I thought they'd work in Baltimore.

He shared his vision for the city and said he felt the police department was broken and in desperate need of fixing.

Finally, we got down to it: he wanted me to interview for the police commissioner's job, although he said there would be other candidates coming in to interview as well.

On my return trip to New York, I was really excited. A chance to be a big-city police commissioner didn't exactly come around every day. Eventually, I thought, it might even lead to my getting the top job in New York – my ultimate dream.

Kate was thrilled for me, but apprehensive, too, about moving to Baltimore. She was originally from California and had moved to New York a few years earlier knowing no one. Now we had just started a family – and I might be asking her to move again?

But the prospect of me essentially having two different incomes, and us living in a far more affordable part of the country, meant she wouldn't have to work and could stay home with Jack. I took to selling that point hard.

"We can actually live like Americans," I told her, "instead of just New Yorkers."

The interview the following weekend back in Baltimore proved to be intense. The interview panel consisted of three people: Bishop Robinson, the former police commissioner and Secretary of the Maryland Department of Public Safety and Corrections; Sean Malone, who would go on to be the police department's chief legal counsel; and attorney Michael Brown.

Now the questions about crime reduction were more pointed and technical. No one sugar-coated how difficult the job would be. For the past 10 years, more than 300 homicides had been recorded annually. Three hundred and five people had been killed in 1999 and over 1,000 of Baltimore's citizens had been shot.

I talked about my philosophy for making a city safer and talked about the tactics that had worked in New York. I stressed the need to have a sizeable police presence in places like East Baltimore and West Baltimore, where the crime numbers were off the charts. But Robinson also asked me my thoughts on policing the Inner Harbor, just to see if I understood that you still had to protect the thousands of tourists who descended there annually.

When it was over, I knew the interview had gone well. Not to brag, but I knew the subject matter better than just about anyone. After all, I had learned how to reduce crime at the foot of the master, Jack Maple. That, to me, was like getting your black belt from Bruce Lee.

Also, I'd been able watch Bill Bratton and Howard Safir run the best police department in the country for years, which meant I'd been exposed to the best leaders and most innovative ideas in law enforcement.

So I knew my stuff. In fact, I'd later find out I was the highest-scoring candidate interviewed.

It didn't matter.

I still didn't get the job.

The next time I sat down with Martin, he laid it out for me in no uncertain terms.

"We just can't have a white mayor and a white police commissioner in this city," he said. It would be too politically combustible, he went on, in a town where African-Americans made up close to 70 percent of the population.

Instead, O'Malley wanted me to take the no. 2 job in the department: Deputy Commissioner, Operations.

Well, thanks, I thought. *But I think I deserve the top spot. And the word is that Seattle, Denver and Los Angeles will all be looking for a new commissioner. And all three are terrific places to live.*

"I already have the operations job in the biggest department in America," I told Martin. "Why would I take the job here?"

But Martin O'Malley wasn't one to give up easily. He had faced long odds in winning the mayor's race and defied the skeptics at every turn. Even *The Washington Post* had seemed flabbergasted when he won the city's hotly-contested Democratic primary, headlining the next day's story with this beauty: "White Man Gets Mayoral Nomination in Baltimore."

No, Martin wasn't about to just shake my hand and say: "OK,

Eddie, thanks for coming down. Have a nice life."

Instead he said: "Let's take a ride."

Moments later, we climbed into the back of an SUV and he took me on a tour of the city. It was late now, going on midnight, as we cruised the darkened streets, Martin making a point of showing me some of the worst neighborhoods.

It was an eye-opening ride, to say the least.

Even at that hour, there were young children out everywhere, toddlers some of them, some with no coats, some with no shoes, despite the cold weather. There was obvious drug-dealing taking place on many blocks and empty crack vials littering the sidewalks and gutters.

At one point, off in the distance, we heard the unmistakable crackle of gunfire.

Jesus, I thought, *what kind of place is this?*

I had worked in some of the roughest parts of New York. But nothing had prepared me for the bleakness that was a place like West Baltimore on a chilly winter night.

"Look," Martin said as we rode along, "I get it. You *should* have a crack at a top job somewhere. But given your talents, where else could you make a bigger impact? This city has the biggest need. I doubt Seattle is as dangerous as this."

Oh, Martin knew how to press your buttons, all right. It was a good argument and it appealed to my sense of duty and my desire to help people, which had only grown stronger from the first day I pulled on a blue uniform.

On the train ride back to Manhattan, I called Kathryn. It wasn't a long conversation.

Taking the No. 2 job in Baltimore, I reasoned, wouldn't really be a step back career-wise. I'd be making decent money ($125,000) and collecting my pension, too. We could actually buy a house now and have a good life in a nice part of the country.

Kathryn was on board. She was willing to take a chance on me – and another new city.

After that, I called Michael Enright. Martin had used a number of football analogies in his sales pitch to me. He'd talked a lot about team-building and needing a quarterback. Whenever he did, though, I'd correct him.

"Hell, you're the mayor," I'd say. "*You're* the quarterback. I'd be the fullback."

Now when I got Enright on the line, I said: "OK, you got yourself a fullback."

It was a momentous decision, probably the biggest of my life. Now I just had to believe it was the right one.

Over the next few weeks, though, I did not exactly wind down my career with the NYPD thumbing through fishing magazines with my feet on the desk.

No, in the waning days of December 1999, the police department – as well as the entire city – was obsessed with what was being called the "Y2K Nightmare."

With the date fast approaching when the calendar would turn from Dec. 31, 1999 to January 1, 2000, it was feared that the world's computers would not be programmed to automatically register a year that began with "20" instead of "19."

Many direly maintained that computer networks would simply shut down, causing catastrophic problems with utility power grids, hospitals, airports, banks, etc.

A number of doomsayers even predicted the end of civilization as we know it. People began withdrawing all their money from ATM's and hoarding food, going into full survivalist mode.

Every day, the NYPD command staff would meet to talk about what terror attacks would come with the Y2K bug, what planes would fall from the sky, what trains and subways would shut down in darkened tunnels or careen off the tracks in smoldering wrecks, what looting hordes would prowl the streets when the lights went out.

We welded manhole covers shut, put snipers with binoculars on rooftops to scan for suspicious activity, installed surveillance cameras everywhere. I had a tremendous responsibility overseeing many of the preparations and was working non-stop.

And then, as the clock struck midnight on New Year's Eve . . . nothing happened.

Well, very little happened, anyway. A few minor technological glitches caused a few machines to shut down, but that was about it.

Civilization did not end. The city was not engulfed in flames. Marauding bands of thugs and killers stayed home. The country woke up the next day with the usual collective big-party hangover, and life went on.

Ten days later I was in Baltimore, eager to begin my new career and the Herculean task of bringing order to what the mayor was calling "the most violent, the most addicted and the most abandoned city in America."

Oh, it sounded like a veritable garden spot, all right.

Tell us how you really feel, Mayor, I thought.

But as I'd soon discover, Martin's bleak description was fitting.

9

The Bloom Comes Off the Rose

After just a few days in Baltimore, I had a serious case of buyer's remorse.

Life was lonely, for one thing. My family was still in Manhattan and I was living alone at the Hyatt downtown, attempting to acclimate myself to this strange new city. I was also working long hours at police headquarters trying to get up to speed with how the department ran.

I had already met the new commissioner, Ronald L. Daniel – Martin O'Malley had sent him up to New York to meet me – and I liked him. Now I was spending a lot of time evaluating the command staff, hoping to determine who the warriors were as opposed to the empty suits, the mopes who were afraid to make decisions, who were just keeping their heads down, putting in their time and hoping for another bullshit promotion.

But the negative vibes I was getting were almost palpable.

It didn't take long to realize that O'Malley was spot-on: the entire department was broken and woefully unprepared for modern-day crime-fighting.

To his credit, Martin had implemented a version of ComStat, the computerized crime-tracking system developed by Jack Maple. But the ComStat meetings here were a far cry from the probing, take-no-prisoners sessions in New York, where precinct commanders and others were interrogated relentlessly and held directly accountable for the crime patterns on their watch.

In Baltimore, only the chief of detectives could ask questions of the detectives. Similarly, only the chief of patrol could grill – and I use that term loosely – patrol officers. The truth was, very little grilling was taking place.

These ComStat meetings featured little more than softball questions lobbed from commanders to staff members, who had clearly been prepped on the subject matter beforehand.

Unlike the heated meetings in New York, here everyone seemed to know the answers to every question. It was absolutely fascinating! No one was ever stumped at all!

Of course, I quickly found out that it was all total bullshit.

During my second Baltimore ComStat meeting, for example, I asked a question about a robbery pattern being discussed.

"What about this guy who's sticking up all the convenience stores?" I said. "What's the status of his case?"

"Well, it's closed," said a detective.

"Oh, good," I replied. "Then the pattern's down. When's the guy's court date?"

"Oh, he hasn't been apprehended," the detective answered. "We haven't arrested him yet."

What?!

Could I have possibly heard that right?

"What do you mean you haven't arrested him?" I demanded.

"Well, I just closed the case," the detective went on. "Meaning he's been identified."

Now the Jack Maple in me came out, the sarcastic, scornful tone my mentor often took when listening to some nervous captain, flop-sweat glistening on his forehead, stammering a mealy-mouth explanation of why he'd failed to do his job properly.

"Ohhhh, OK, I get it now," I said. "So you have his *picture*. So you're going to put his *picture* in a shoebox with the *pictures* of the other crooks, so he'll be in shoebox jail? Is that what we're gonna do with this guy?"

Everyone in the room cracked up. Well, *almost* everyone. I could see the commanders looking uneasily at each other. They weren't real happy with me. Nevertheless, they got the message: the case isn't closed until the arrest is made. No one would forget that going forward.

There was also a relaxed, we'll-get-to-it-when-we-get-to-it attitude permeating the Baltimore PD that I found unsettling.

One day early in my tenure, I was in my office around noon when the police radio squawked: "Man with a machinegun in Patterson Park . . ."

I had only been in town a couple of weeks and had no idea where Patterson Park was. Nevertheless, I jumped up, grabbed my hat – I dressed in full uniform again – and ran down to the patrol side of headquarters.

There I found the chief of patrol and his staff members sitting in their office, calmly eating lunch.

"There's a guy with a machine gun in Patterson Park!" I said. "Let's go!"

No one made a move to get up.

"Yeah, we know," someone said.

I looked at them incredulously. And I said it again, this time louder and more slowly: "THERE'S A GUY . . . IN ONE OF OUR PARKS . . . WITH A MACHINE GUN! DOES THIS HAPPEN EVERY DAY AROUND HERE? ISNT THIS KIND OF A BIG DEAL? LET'S GO!"

Clearly, they were bent on finishing their lunch.

I guess they were thinking: *Well, the precinct closest to the park will take that gun call.* Which was true, of course. But, my God, this was the chief of patrol not making a move to respond! When he was only a few miles away, too!

I was horrified. As I would say over and over during my time in Baltimore, I believe in leading from the front, not from headquarters.

What kind of example was this top commander setting for his troops?

As it turned out, the man in the park didn't have a machine gun after all – he had a rifle. But it didn't matter at all to my way of thinking.

Let's go over it again: there was a guy with a long gun in a public park.

At noon.

On a busy weekday.

This wasn't just some scumbag with a gun at three in the morning on the corner of Monroe and Fayette streets. This was a potential disaster in the making in a park. That chief of patrol and his men, I concluded, had different priorities than I did.

Very different.

Underlying this reluctance to get off their asses was an attitude that seemed prevalent throughout headquarters: *Hey, the police work is done by policemen. We work at headquarters – we're administrative guys.*

I vowed that way of thinking was going to change. I let my people know I wanted to see them in the street, which was one of the reasons I went on patrol every day.

In the days and weeks ahead, it seemed that everywhere I looked in the department, there was a major problem.

Once, I asked to see what kind of wiretap and active cases we had going.

"We have no wiretaps, sir," was the reply.

Ohhh-kay. Baltimore has the biggest drug problem in America – and we're not tapping any phones?

What about surveillance vans? I asked. And video cameras to monitor drug trafficking corridors?

"We don't have any, sir."

OK, I said, what about helicopters? *Please* tell me we have helicopters . . .

"No helicopters, sir," was the answer.

What I learned was that there had been a tragic accident involving the police chopper, known as Foxtrot, a year earlier. It had spiraled out of the sky due to a mechanical failure and crashed into the B&O Railroad Museum downtown.

The flight officer at the controls had been killed. The aerial observer with him had been seriously injured.

Yet instead of trying to find out what had caused the accident – and how to prevent another in the future – they had scrapped the whole program!

Now, one of the biggest police departments in the whole country was without an aviation unit. How could that possibly be?

Photo arrays were another area in which the Baltimore PD seemed positively medieval. When you have a criminal suspect to be identi-fied by a victim, you put the suspect's photo in an array with five other photos showing people of similar appearance. In policing, this is known as a "six-pack."

But this was not the procedure being followed in Baltimore. Here, they were showing crime victims paper photos out of shoeboxes and photo albums, the kind you'd buy at Wahlgreens. And the photos were of every variety – color, black-and-white, Polaroids – in all dif-ferent shapes and sizes.

In terms of how backward this was, it was like doctors still using leeches to treat infections.

Holy shit! I thought. *This place is totally dysfunctional!*

What else was wrong? There were 250 people wanted for murder or attempted murder in Baltimore, and exactly three officers looking for them in the warrant division. Meanwhile, we had 90 officers help-ing run the Police Athletic League, which was nationally known and extremely popular with both the cops and the citizens.

Understand, I was a big supporter of the PAL centers. Hey, I had been a PAL kid myself growing up. The PAL center was where I had learned to box. But in a city faced with the fifth- highest homicide rate in the country and a heroin epidemic that had produced some 60,000 addicts, devoting 90 cops to essentially baby-sitting kids all day and shooting baskets with them was a twisted priority, in my view.

"Congratulations," I said to the PAL people. "You have the best PAL program in the country because the streets are so dangerous, you have to lock the kids inside."

So I promptly closed some PAL centers. And people were not happy with me. But I saw PAL as a social services agency, not a police agency.

I had heard that the previous commissioner, Thomas Frazier, a California transplant, had said he felt police were essentially social workers with guns. But I didn't agree with that philosophy. In fact, I hated it. So I used the freed-up manpower from the PAL program to start the department's first dedicated warrant squad.

In addition to some of the archaic and misguided ways in which the Baltimore police operated, there was also a culture of vengeance within the department that was unnerving

This was a score-settling place worthy of a mob family. When I got here, people loyal to the previous police administration were being summarily fired before the new commanders had even settled into their desks and put up photos of their kids.

In New York, I had always been loyal to the commissioner's chair – the *position* of commissioner, if not the actual person who held it. But here, people deemed loyal to the previous administration were canned immediately, no matter how talented and dedicated they were.

The forced resignation of Colonel Margaret ("Maggie") Patten showed me just how vicious these department coups could be.

Patten, 52, was a 26-year veteran of the force and a tireless advocate for the victims of domestic violence in the community. Extremely effective and popular within the ranks, she had nevertheless been asked to leave by incoming commissioner Ron Daniel.

The night after she got whacked, I was on patrol. When I pulled into the police parking lot around 11, my headlights caught the administrative deputy commissioner and a sergeant jumping up and down and yelling like crazy men.

What the hell? I wondered.

It turned out that they had just ripped down the metal sign for Maggie Patten's parking spot, and were now gleefully stomping on it in celebration.

As the expression goes, sometimes there are no words. I just shook my head, walked into the building and headed to my office.

Where in God's name am I? I wondered. I couldn't picture any executive in the NYPD *ever* doing what I had just witnessed. No, commanders there didn't get to the top by being nice guys all the time. But most were pretty dignified. I couldn't imagine any of them ripping down parking signs and jumping on them like school kids.

But no matter how lonely I was in Baltimore, or how depressing the new job seemed at times, the fact was: I wasn't going anywhere else.

I couldn't go home to New York – my old job had already been filled. And since I was the deputy commissioner of ops in Baltimore and not the commissioner, I couldn't really change a lot about the culture of the department without the approval of my boss.

For the time being anyway, I was going to have to make the best of it. And I would do what I came here to do, which was to help make the citizens of America's 19th largest city safer.

It sure as hell wouldn't be easy, though, as I was reminded on one of my very first days on the job.

"Show me around the city," I had asked a member of my security detail. "And I don't want to see the Inner Harbor or the stadiums. I want to see the bad areas. That's the reason I'm here. So show me the toughest places in town."

We went for a ride in a marked car, with me in the passenger seat. It was a bright sunny day and I was in full uniform, wearing my hat, when we pulled up to a busy corner in East Baltimore.

I looked to my right and saw a cluster of men in their 30's and 40's gathered on the sidewalk. Clearly there was a drug deal going down. Or as we say in court: "From my experience as a police officer, Your

Honor, it looked like a hand-to-hand drug sale."

Now, part of what you do every day as a cop in a drug neighborhood is this: you pull up to a corner, give the dealers a look, and they run. Or at least they move on.

They give you some respect. But on this particular day, one of the dealers apparently wasn't playing that game. Instead, I looked at him, he looked at me – and then he went back to transacting business!

Did I mention all this was taking place in broad daylight?

And I was in a *marked* police car?

Wearing a uniform and hat with enough gold braid to make me look like a Mexican general?

But this dealer was totally unfazed. He looked so comfortable, you'd think him and his buddies were trading baseball cards. Or exchanging Tupperware.

I flung the door open and flew out of the car. Now everyone on the corner started to run in different directions. But I caught the guy who'd been staring at me, who was apparently the slowest dealer of the group, maybe the slowest in Baltimore.

As I tackled him and we fell to the ground, he started frantically stuffing something into his mouth. I grabbed him by the throat, reached into his mouth, and yanked out some heroin gel capsules.

After I cuffed him, I got right in his face.

"Dude," I said, "what the fuck? You don't give me any respect? I'm in full uniform, I got gold all over me and you don't run? You stand there and make me look like an asshole?"

Now the guy wore a sheepish look.

"Well," he said, "a lot of times the *poh-leece* ride by and don't do anything. So I thought you were just going to ride by."

The guy was telling the truth. I *knew* he was telling the truth. And it was a sobering moment for me.

Wow, I thought, *Baltimore has really raised the white flag when it comes to drugs and crime. The city has totally surrendered. Can I really hope to change the culture of this place? Or is it too far gone at this point for anyone to make a difference?*

In any event, word of the new deputy commissioner of operations running down a "corner boy" and arresting him spread rapidly across the city.

When I got back to the office, a reporter from the *Baltimore Sun* called, asking for details. And the next day there was an article in the newspaper chronicling the heroics of the city's new no. 2 cop

It was framed as a bit of a man-bites-dog story: top police honcho deigns to actually leave his patrol car and dirty his uniform wrestling with a dope dealer! Who had ever heard of such a thing!

Soon my take-down of the dealer was all over TV, too. Oh, well. At least I had made a good first impression with my fellow police officers and a fair number of Baltimoreans.

I'd need every bit of that good will just a few months later, when the politics of saving America's most dangerous city would devour yet another good and decent man.

10

"You Sit Like a Racist"

In the weeks that followed, a good deal of my gloom lifted as I adopted a new philosophy. It was almost laser-like, if not Zen-like, in its focus: I would concentrate only on matters I could control within the police department, which was the crime side, the operational side.

The drug war, I thought, was unwinnable. It was ridiculous and a waste of everyone's time and money and blood. But I knew how to reduce crime quickly. It was no big secret. We had done it in New York and we could do it here. And the key, once again, would be fugitive enforcement.

First I decided to concentrate on catching the predatory core of criminals wreaking havoc on Baltimore. You're not going to rid the street corners of drugs anytime soon in America. But we could do something about the thugs wanted for crimes.

It was the easiest, most effective way to make an impact. When people already have warrants on them, they've already been indicted for a crime. So you don't have to develop a case. All you have to do is find out where they sleep. That's it.

To help track down the 250 fugitives we had wanted for murder or attempted murder, I met first with the U.S. Marshal's Service. That's what they do for a living. Sure, they protect courthouses and judges. But what they're really known for, going back to the days of the Old West, is chasing fugitives. That's their history. That's their biggest source of pride.

They gave us tremendous cooperation and lent us a lot of deputy marshals. The collaboration was so successful that I decided to hit up the FBI and Secret Service, as well as the surrounding counties, to help us track down bad guys, too.

In addition to that, I knew we had to beef up the ComStat system, too. The rehearsed questions and the even more scripted answers at our weekly meetings were getting us nowhere.

ComStat was not supposed to be theater. It wasn't designed to be a feel-good pageant, so that everyone in the room left thinking: "Yeah, we really grilled them today, boss!" It was devised to be a real management tool to figure out what was causing crime in the districts.

Also, it gave commanders a chance to – for lack of a better word – audition their employees. It was a great exercise for an ambitious police officer to show what he or she was made of, too. In what other line of work do you get a chance to stand up in front of the CEO every week to show how smart you are?

Or how stupid.

Yes, it's a powerful tool that can work either way. But if you're good, you *want* to stand up in front of the boss. *Let me show him what I think* should be your mindset. *'Cause I know these other mopes in the room are just faking it.*

But this brutally honest back and forth was lacking at our ComStat meetings.

The crime assessments rang false. It was as if you were showing someone a major league baseball game for the first time, except the pitcher's only throwing it 60 miles an hour right down the middle of the plate and every batter is knocking it out of the park.

That's not how the game's really played! But our earliest ComStat meetings in Baltimore were equally artificial. They were a Potemkin village of what the real thing should look like.

Commanders weren't prepared. The questions weren't probative. Supervisors would prepare to be questioned on one subject and one subject alone, such as robberies, when I wanted them to address *every-thing* under their command: burglaries, shootings, prostitutes on the corner, you name it.

The four basic tenets of ComStat – accurate and timely intelligence, rapid deployment, effective tactics and relentless follow-up and assessment – that's what I was trying to teach.

Understand, I had nothing but compassion for precinct commanders, because they were responsible for everything. They got shit from the community, they got shit from their officers, they got shit from me.

But sometimes I just wanted to scream at the incompetence shown during these meetings.

I would bring in the head of the auto larceny task force, for example. And the conversation would go something like this:

Me: "What's the most frequently-stolen vehicle in Baltimore?"

Him: "I don't know."

Me: "Well, where are they taking them?'

Him: "I don't know."

Me: "Are they stealing them for parts? Are they shipping them out of the country? Where are they stealing them from?"

Him: "I . . . I don't know."

Now he's stammering and sweating and thoroughly humiliated.

OK, I'd think. *Now I'm going to teach you how to do this…*

"You start to plot where your cars are stolen and where they're recovered," I'd explain. "You can't hide cars like dead bodies, unless you're cutting them up and shipping them out in containers. In that case, where are the chop shops?

"And use the computers! You have all these reports of cars stolen by vehicle type and time of day. Put them in the computer! You know where it was recovered. Put it in the computer! Let's say 50 cars have been found in the same location within a few miles' radius. There's probably a road between where they were taken and where they were found. Set up there!"

Oh, God, I would get so frustrated in my early days on my new job! As it happened, I wasn't the only one being driven to wit's end.

Ron Daniel, the new commissioner, was having a tough time, too, only for an entirely different reason. Martin, in his zeal to get the police department up to speed and make good on his campaign promise to slash the crime rate, was micro-managing Ron to death.

In our daily conversations, I could see Ron getting more and more beaten down.

"I *cannot* get my work done," he'd say of Martin. "The man is driving me crazy."

Ron said that Martin would call him all day, every day, wanting to know about this new shooting or that new case that a city councilman was bugging him about. It was as if the new mayor had suddenly decided he wanted to be the new police chief, too.

"I don't know how much more I can take," Ron would say mournfully. "I don't know if I'm going to stay."

"You *can't* quit!" I would yell. "I just moved here! I'm not working for somebody else!"

At the time, I didn't think I had a chance in hell of replacing Ron as the new commissioner if he stepped down. I hadn't been here long, but I'd already gotten a quick taste of the racial racketeering that was going on in Baltimore.

No one on the City Council, or in the African-American community organizations or the churches, would want me in that post.

A white guy from New York City with a thick accent replacing a popular black commissioner who'd been a 27-year fixture in the department?

Uh-uh. Not going to happen.

No, my fear was that if Ron left, I'd be out of a job. The new commissioner would want to name his own second in command. And Eddie Norris, having just moved his pretty wife and infant son from his hometown, would be hung out to dry.

Yet after only 57 days on the job, Ron Daniel finally had enough of Martin's antics and abruptly resigned in March of 2000.

"Ron Daniel and I both share a commitment to make Baltimore a safer place," Martin announced in a masterful job of soft-soaping the news to the press. "But we have come to the conclusion that our differences in how to get the job done make it impossible for us to collaborate in achieving that common goal."

Daniel's resignation sent shock waves through both the city and the police department.

City hall sources told the *Baltimore Sun* that, in addition to have Martin on his butt constantly, Daniel simply couldn't work with Jack Maple and John Linder, who were still doing crime consulting for the city at Martin's behest.

In a damning report by the Maple/Linder team released that month, the city was found to have "a police culture characterized by cynicism and distrust"; "unreliable and poorly-designed data systems"; "little, if any, discussion about crime trends in command meetings or during roll calls"; "an extraordinary number" of complaints about police conduct and awful morale among officers because of the department's "tarnished reputation."

Yet, the *Sun* reported: "When the Maple/Linder group offered 87 suggestions for how to reduce crime in Baltimore, Daniel rejected half."

Other sources, according to the *Sun*, blamed both O'Malley's impatience and "Daniel's history of bucking authority" for the break-up, suggesting it had been a toxic mix from the beginning.

Whatever the reason for Ron's departure, my phone rang later that day, with Martin summoning me to City Hall. When I got there, the media was already camped outside, the whiff of another big story creating the usual frenzy.

Martin told me I was now in charge of the department – the acting commissioner, at least for the time being. He said he still didn't think the city would go for a white police chief. Yet he talked about wanting me to stay on no matter who was eventually named commissioner.

But I was having none of it.

Even though I thought the mayor's reading of Baltimore's racial landscape was undoubtedly correct, I had nothing to lose at this point. If they were going to start interviewing for the top job, white man or no white man, I at least wanted to be considered.

"Look," I said, "I agreed to work for Ron Daniel. I didn't agree to work for just 'some guy.' I was fine working for him. But I'm not going to work for a total stranger now that you're going to plop someone over me for racial reasons.

"I'm a qualified candidate," I continued. "In fact, I was your *most* qualified candidate, according to what I heard. I deserve a shot at this job now. If not, I'm going to go."

Martin, to his ever-lasting credit, finally agreed to go to bat for me as the next police commissioner.

We both knew it would be a damn tough sell. A hard-working, well-liked black chief stepping down – no, *forced out*, the critics would say – with a white assistant commissioner conveniently waiting in the wings to take his place, would set off a political firestorm.

Martin was already getting hammered by many in the black community for his "zero tolerance" policing, decried as brutal and racist. Thankfully, Ron Daniel didn't lash out at Martin when he resigned, leaving as professionally and courteously as he had comported himself throughout his career. But there was a huge outcry in the black community over his perceived mistreatment.

With City Hall in full crisis mode, Martin began working the City Council hard on my behalf. He used up a lot of favors, burned a lot of political capital. With the help of Jack Maple and John Linder, I quickly came up with a plan, a codified document, of how I planned to reduce crime in the city.

It did not exactly have a catchy name.

"The Plan to Dramatically Reduce Crime in Baltimore," as we called it, was originally drawn up on cocktail napkins in a hotel bar as Jack, John and I huddled feverishly night after night. It involved everything from fugitive enforcement to beefing up our technology with wire-tap capabilities and cellular phone tracking to bringing back helicopters and acquiring surveillance vans.

I also wanted pay raises for the department as a morale booster. We were paying our police laughable wages, way less than the county agencies and the State Police were paying their employees. As a result, we were losing our best people; experienced investigators and trained snipers were leaving year after year.

Now, armed with a bound copy of "The Plan," we set off to sell the idea of me as the next police commissioner to the good people of Baltimore.

It was an absolutely draining task.

For weeks we appeared at town hall meetings in auditoriums at various schools throughout the city. At each event, I would get up before the question-and-answer segment and go over the details of how we proposed to bring order to the city. These were often heated, chaotic sessions that lasted for hours, with Martin and I seated on the stage as citizens took the microphones one by one, to grill us.

Some questions were legitimate and probing; others, prefaced by long, angry screeds, were more agitprop than anything else.

We took a good deal of abuse, as we knew we would, with some of the same professional agitators showing up at each event to inflame the crowd, insisting that the plot all along was to get Ron Daniel fired so a white guy could take over as Baltimore's top cop.

At one raucous meeting, someone yelled at me: "You were involved in the Amadou Diallo shooting!"

"No, I was not," I said.

Firmly, I explained I had nothing to do with the infamous case of the 23-year-old immigrant from Guinea who was shot 41 times by four plainclothes officers in the Bronx a year earlier, an incident which set off a firestorm of controversy nationwide over alleged police brutality and racial profiling.

"You look like a racist!" a black woman shouted.

Another black woman nearby turned on the person who had just shouted and barked: "What do you mean he looks like a racist?! Shut your mouth!"

"Well," the first woman grumbled, "he *sits* like a racist!"

We lobbied in front of the City Council, too, and in front of the state delegation in Annapolis. I was working all day, attending these meetings in the evenings and somehow existing on three hours of sleep a night.

But I was a true believer in what we were doing. And I knew the fate of the city hung in the balance.

"There's a crisis going on here," I said on a local radio talk show. "The mayor won the election with a 'zero tolerance' program. That tells me a lot of people are tired of having people standing in their neighborhood selling drugs openly."

Addressing the concerns of the African-American community, I made it clear we weren't just going to start locking up people who were littering or urinating in alleys. We were going to use targeted enforcement to attack the bad guys who were creating specific problems in city neighborhoods.

Right now, I said, the lack of leadership in the department was destroying the morale of the 3,188 sworn officers, which in turn was endangering the lives of Baltimore residents.

For weeks, we pressed on in our campaign to convince lawmakers and citizens alike that I was the best man for the job. Martin launched a full-blown letter-writing campaign, sending out some 28,000 pieces of mail to residents.

But I was also getting angry and frustrated with this Kafkaesque process of begging people to let me save lives.

"You know," I said to Martin, during one of my lowest moments, "I have a better chance of being an astronaut than I do of becoming the police chief here."

At a meeting with the state delegation in Annapolis, one of the African-American lawmakers took me aside for a few words.

"We know you're the most qualified candidate," he said. "But we were expecting a different, um, hue."

I became so angry, the top of my head nearly exploded.

"Really?" I said. "If the guy who can save more black lives in the city is white, you don't want me? Because I'm not black?"

Finally, though, the arduous campaign came to an end and all our hard work paid off.

On the night of May 8, 2000, I was unanimously confirmed by the City Council to be the new police commissioner. And nearly three weeks later, with Kathryn and 10-month-old Jack at my side, I was sworn in during a public ceremony at the War Memorial Building, after which I was given a standing ovation.

"It was a long process and a difficult time for the Police Department and this city," I told the crowd. "I will certainly show you that you made the right decision."

Remembering my astronaut line, Martin gave me the gift of a model rocket as an inside joke. It would be something I would keep for years.

After that it was time to roll up our sleeves and make good on our promises.

In a majority black city, a white mayor and a white police chief were now leading the fight to pull Baltimore out of the long death spiral it had been in for over a decade.

Our grand "Plan to Reduce Crime" was about to be tested in the dangerous drug-infested streets in a big way.

God help us all if it didn't work.

11

Batman and Robin Bring Hope

"The Plan" might have been the dullest-sounding policy paper on earth, but the mandate from City Hall was to implement it at break-neck speed. The pressure to do something about the violent crime ruining life in so many of Baltimore's poorest neighborhoods was constant and overwhelming.

"Eddie had a high level of energy," my chief of staff, John Stendrini, told a reporter, "because things had to be done quickly."

One of my first moves was to petition the local business community to create the Baltimore Police Foundation, which would help us buy much-needed equipment we couldn't purchase under the city's tight budget.

A big priority was finding a way to run the department from the field in the event of a terrorist incident. This was a year before the horrendous Sept. 11 terrorist attacks that would shake the country to its core. But terrorism had been on my mind for a long time, certainly since the days of the Meir Kahane assassination and the revelations of El Sayyid Nosair's ties to a shadowy network of Middle Eastern and Islamist radicals.

America's enemies, I knew, were constantly studying our nation's security systems and probing for weak spots to exploit. To operate the department remotely in case of a direct attack on the city and our headquarters, we used Police Foundation money to buy a big, million-dollar RV, which we painted black and named our Mobile Command Vehicle.

At the time, it was the most technologically-loaded vehicle in the country. From it, we could run every facet of the department. We would go on to use the vehicle for many different functions, such as monitoring big events – like the annual Fourth of July celebrations – at the Inner Harbor and responding to hostage situations.

I also brought back something that was decidedly low- tech: the espantoon, the traditional Baltimore nightstick so beloved by most of the force. Thomas Frazier, my predecessor, had felt the age-old practice of cops twirling the heavy nightstick was intimidating to citizens.

So he'd replaced the espantoons with something called Koga sticks, longer and lighter batons which could be used in conjunction with the martial arts to subdue the bad guys. But espantoons had been used by Baltimore cops since the turn of the century, and many had seen Frazier's move as the further eroding of the traditions of a once-proud police department.

During this time, I'd have lunches with the city's movers and shakers, such as Baltimore Orioles' owner Peter G. Angelos and bakery mogul/developer John Paterakis Sr., to wrangle money for such necessities as K-9 dogs, bulletproof vests and saddles for our mounted patrols.

I was hitting up everybody I could think of, doing my song and dance about items we needed to make the city safer.

Martin and I went to Washington D.C. and talked to Eric Holder, then the U.S. Deputy Attorney General, about getting funding from the Community Oriented Policing Services (COPS) program to hire more police and provide raises for existing officers.

Hard-charging doesn't begin to explain the mindset I brought to the job in those first months. Going after bad guys on the run, targeting high crime areas, beefing up our ComStat system, fund-raising for better, more modern equipment, improving the morale of the department with raises – all of it began to have a noticeable effect on

Baltimore's crime statistics.

At a news conference at the Inner Harbor, I pulled a page from Joe Namath's Super Bowl III scrapbook and guaranteed we'd drive the homicide rate under 300 for the first time in a decade. (It was 305 the year I took over.)

Reporters rolled their eyes and laughed. Members of my command staff had a similar reaction.

This is Baltimore, they thought. *He doesn't know. It's never going to work.*

I never mentioned an explicit number as our goal. The truth was, I was never comfortable thinking of the city's homicide epidemic in numeric terms.

To me, these homicide victims weren't just brown folders that went in a file cabinet. These were real people, many of whom had been cut down in the prime of their lives and had left behind grieving families that would be forever shattered. If you framed all this simply in terms of numbers, it de-humanized the killings even further.

Martin O'Malley heard about my prediction of a sub-300 year for homicides and liked it – mainly, I think, because my soaring confidence gave him a shot of confidence, too.

"If you just believe in me and let me do my job," I would promise him, "crime is going to go down."

Martin was totally on board with my Namath-like bluster to the press.

A friend of mine had just returned from a trip to Ireland, and had brought me a bottle of *poitin*, or Irish moonshine. Martin and I agreed that if we finished the year with fewer than 300 homicides by New Year's Eve, we would celebrate with a belt of the poitin. He squirreled the bottle away at City Hall for safe-keeping.

As that first year rolled on, we continued to make progress. But there were plenty of rough patches, too.

That May, I fired four high-ranking commanders. Two were African-American and two were white. But when the *Baltimore Sun* trumpeted the story in the next day's newspaper, the photos of the black officers appeared on the front page, while the white officers were pictured on the jump page inside.

Guess who was promptly – and predictably – called a racist?

But the story behind the firings – it couldn't have been more bizarre, more thoroughly Baltimore – was this: a lieutenant had been taking his departmental car home at night while not authorized to do so. And someone eventually ratted him out.

But instead of simply investigating the officer and disciplining him, Deputy Police Commissioner Barry Powell and Col. James L. Hawkins, the two black officers, took it upon themselves to take a spare set of car keys and drive to the lieutenant's house in Carroll County.

Instead of simply observing the car in the driveway and taking pictures of it – which should have rightfully been a job for a detective from Internal Affairs – they used their spare keys to steal the car. Then they drove it back to Baltimore, abandoned it on Northern Parkway and placed a call to 911 – using the worst fake voice in history – to report the location of the car.

The entire charade was done because the two men wanted either the lieutenant or his commanding officer, a good cop named John Bergbower, fired. Except the faux, stuttering voice on the 911 recording was quickly recognized as Hawkins,' and the plot unraveled just as fast when Powell was alleged to have known about the caper.

When I heard what had happened, I summoned Powell and Hawkins to my office and laced into them.

"What the fuck?" I yelled. "How many bodies a day do we have dropping in this town? And this is what we're concerned about?"

To me, a shake-up was clearly needed. To the howls of the City Council, I got rid of both of officers, along with two white officers who were also contributing to the culture of vengeance in a department where, as *Sun* columnist Gregory Kane noted: "scores get settled with old enemies and favors are handed out to friends."

Unfortunately, the embarrassing incident cost the department dearly. Bergbower, 49, and the head of our important Regional Warrant Apprehension Task Force, soon resigned over the flap, yet another victim of the sharp-elbowed vindictiveness rife within the agency.

I tried to persuade him to stay on. But he was too hurt and disgusted over the histrionics of Powell and Hawkins to change his mind.

Another officer eventually forced out was an African-American lieutenant named John M. Mack, a 17-year veteran of the department who was discovered providing muscle for a bunch of pimps. He was essentially running a floating whorehouse, an operation that would set up shop in empty bars and clubs to provide patrons with booze, drugs and prostitutes.

This, of course, was the worst kind of corruption imaginable: actively cooperating in a criminal endeavor. Martin O'Malley and I had both promised to clean up the department; it was one of our core missions. But when the City Council got wind that I had fired the pimp-friendly cop, they summoned me to a meeting and pressured me to bring him back.

I was astonished and angry that they would question my judgment and waste my time over such an egregious case of police misconduct. My sarcasm, which had been simmering throughout the meeting, finally bubbled to the surface.

"You know, you're right," I told the council members. "On second thought, I *will* hire Lt. Mack back."

Now you could see the wary looks on their faces: *You will?*

"I just need to know who wants him in their district," I continued.

Now I went around the room, pointing at individual members.

"Do you want him, Councilman?" I said. "How about you? I'll put him in your district tomorrow. What about you over there?"

No one responded, of course. Suddenly, all the members were looking down at their shoes or developing a renewed fascination for the paperwork in front of them.

With that, I reached for my hat and motioned to my command staff.

"We're leaving," I said. And that's exactly what we did.

On the walk back to my office, one of my staff members marveled at how I'd been able to back down the once-angry council members.

"When I get home," he said, "I'm gonna drink a big glass of testosterone."

Sure, he was kidding. But the fact was, an industrial-strength shot of that stuff was often what you needed in this job to fight for what was right.

We did the same thing to root out corruption in the internal affairs unit – and ran into stumbling blocks there, too.

When an officer named Brian L. Sewell was caught up in a drug sting and indicted on charges of criminal perjury and misconduct, a secret internal affairs office in Dundalk was burglarized and trashed three months later, and the evidence in his case was taken.,

This totally freaked me out. It showed the level of corruption in the department and the utter lack of concern among the participants about being discovered. The message was clear: *We're not afraid of any-body. We're not afraid of you, Commissioner. And we're sure as hell not afraid of internal affairs.*

Sure enough, the case was soon dropped by the state's attorney Patricia Jessamy, causing Martin to go ballistic and me to wonder, once again, at the culture of lawlessness all around me.

Combine all this with the crime wave we were facing, and the sheer brutality playing out on the streets, and the challenges that year were enormous.

Nevertheless, in December of 2000, we were holding our breath as the number of homicides held at around 260. A terrible month with 40-some killings, we knew, could still push that number over 300.

Not only would it make my boasts ring hollow, we would take a significant PR hit in our effort to convince the citizens that Baltimore was now a safer place.

But as the New Year was rung in, it was official: for the first time in more than a decade, the city had recorded fewer than 300 homicides. In a year that had begun with a bloody spate of killings that had surpassed the previous year's pace by nearly three dozen, Baltimore had finished with 262 homicides.

Martin and I were euphoric.

"It's a tremendous morale boost to the Police Department," I told reporters, noting that 262 killings were still "a terrible number. It's nothing to do back-flips over. It doesn't make us the safest city in the country. But it shows that we can make a big difference.

"Now," I added, "we look at the next big milestone: 200."

As promised, Martin and I celebrated in his office by cracking open the bottle of Irish hooch. (Joining us in a toast, interestingly enough, was Catherine Pugh, who was a member of the City Council at the time and is now Baltimore's new mayor.)

A celebratory drink seemed appropriate. It had been a heady first year for the team the newspaper was now calling "Batman and Robin."

Things were certainly looking up for Eddie Norris. Crime was going down. The mayor loved me; it seemed as if the whole city did, too. Soon I was listed in *CEO* magazine in a feature on the 10 toughest executives in the state.

Another on the list was Baltimore Orioles' owner and super-litigator Peter G. Angelos, who was quoted as saying of me: "I get the impression he's going somewhere, he's going quick and he's taking us with him."

Hell, I was the greatest thing since Cal Ripken, Jr. We were making a ton of arrests. And the naysayers who predicted citizen outrage over our tough, no-nonsense, "zero-tolerance" or "targeted enforcement" approach to crime, were mostly silent.

Going into 2001, we had a lot of momentum on our side. In May, the *Baltimore Sun* ran an editorial titled: "Ed Norris' first year shows gains in policing."

"The dirty little secret among criminologists is that no one quite knows why crime goes up or down," it began. "Virtually the only thing that can be statistically proved is that when crime dips because of crackdowns, citizen complaints against police tend to skyrocket.

"That's why Edward T. Norris' first year as Baltimore's police commissioner is impressive," it continued. "An all-out policing effort has helped curb the city's shockingly high homicide rate without triggering a wave of complaints about excessive law enforcement tactics.

"This is particularly gratifying because alarmists predicted the opposite just a year ago. They argued Mr. Norris' New York training and background . . . virtually guaranteed he would employ cowboy tactics to suppress crime."

I was working my ass off, putting in long hours and then showing up at shootings at 3 in the morning to tell cops they had done a good job. They definitely were not used to that.

During an attempted stick-up of a bar in the Northeast District on a Sunday afternoon, police responded and shot one of the criminals when he raised his gun at them. When the two cops involved in the shooting were brought down to homicide to be de-briefed, I went to talk to them.

As soon as I walked in the room, they jumped up and started apologizing.

"So sorry, sir!" one of them blurted. "We just *had* to shoot and . . ."

"What are you apologizing for?" I said. "I'm just coming here to say 'Good job' and to make sure you're OK. I know it's traumatic to be involved in these things."

It was clearly not the reaction they expected. No, the reaction they expected was the usual angry condemnation: Why'd you fire? Take their guns, suspend them, investigate them, etc.

Around this time, too, we had a young officer arrest a suspect in the suspect's home on an arson warrant. As soon as the suspect was handcuffed, he told the officer: "I gotta pee."

This, you should know, is a routine ploy. Every time somebody's cuffed, the first thing you hear from them is: "I gotta pee! I gotta pee!"

The inexperienced cop fell for it. He un-cuffed the man and allowed him to go relieve himself, a major tactical error.

After a minute or two, the officer went to check on him. When he pushed open the bathroom door, he found the suspect cutting his wrists with a kitchen knife. The man then lunged at the officer with the knife. But the cop managed to draw his service weapon, and shot and killed the man.

When I got to the scene of the incident, a large angry crowd had already gathered outside. Rumors of what had happened were circulating everywhere.

After I was briefed on the details, I went in front of the TV cameras. Right away, the reporters were demanding to know if the officer had committed a violation of department procedure.

"We're going to investigate that and he'll be disciplined for it if he's found guilty of violating any procedure," I said. "But if you jump at *me* with a knife in a tight hallway, I'm going to kill you, too."

The upshot was that police officers now knew they were being supported by their new commissioner. I wasn't going to throw them under the bus every time someone accused them of something.

I was winning the rank-and-file over in another important way, too.

For months, the FBI had been investigating some 20 city police officers – along with a few Baltimore County officers – who had been moonlighting at a Staples. The allegations were that the cops had been working as security guards at the office supply store while also supposedly on-duty. The feds also wanted to know if the cops were being paid for work they never performed.

The investigation finally seemed to be coming to a head. I got a call from the FBI saying, essentially: "Look, we're indicting these officers. You better suspend them."

"I'm not doing it," I told them. "You indict them, I'll suspend them. But until that day comes, I'm not doing it."

Baltimore County would end up suspending their officers involved in the case, but I didn't suspend mine. And eventually, after a two-year federal investigation, prosecutors declined to press charges and quietly dropped the case.

Over and over, I began hearing how the rank-and-file of the department were grateful for my support. But how could I *not* have their backs?

Being a police officer, I knew, was a job unlike any other. With this job, the best thing officers do every day is risk their lives for strangers who might not even like them. As a commissioner, therefore, you really have to know how to motivate people. And one way is to offer them all the encouragement and reassurance you can when they're doing their jobs correctly, and with passion and diligence.

Long ago I learned it's just as easy for an officer to be the fourth car at the scene of a crime as the first car. So if it's a disgruntled officer who's supposed to be racing to save someone's life or respond to a report of a man with a gun, he might think: *Fuck it, the department's not going to support us. So I'm not doing my job and risking my neck.*

Given the aggressive policing I was demanding, it was more important than ever that officers knew I'd back them to the hilt.

When, for example, I heard there was a tradition of people in the city shooting guns in the air when the clock struck midnight on New Year's Eve, I was appalled.

"What do you *do* about this?" I asked some of my officers.

"Well," they said, "we're told to wait in the parking lot until five minutes after midnight."

The message from previous commanders was clear: don't get involved. Stay inside until the bullets stop falling from the sky. Don't rock the boat.

"No, we're not doing that anymore," I said. "We're not hiding. We're the *police*. We're getting *involved*."

I went out on patrol that first New Year's Eve and within a couple minutes after midnight, three police shootings had already been reported. And from the entire tour that night we confiscated 121 guns throughout the city.

I was in a really good place mentally at this point. I was pushing as hard as possible to help turn the city around, and not for political aspirations. I wasn't looking for the next job.

No, I'm one of those people who are cursed, because I'm a true believer. I really believe in this stuff. I knew I could make a difference in the life of this city. And best of all, what we were doing was working.

But 2001 would also become one of the saddest years of my life, as my best friend, Jack Maple, was losing his battle with colon cancer. I was routinely driving up to New York after work to see him at Memorial Sloan-Kettering Cancer Center, and watching him wither away was agonizing.

Yet his basic personality never changed. He remained a character right up to the end.

One day when Bill Bratton and I visited Jack in his hospital room, Bratton asked gently: "Jack, is there anything I can do for you?"

Jack thought about it for a moment.

"Yeah," he said at last, "*you* can have cancer."

Jack finally passed away in August of that year. I took his death very hard. I was working my ass off. The days were long, crammed with staff meetings, cabinet meetings and meetings with the NAACP, in addition to me going out on patrol and also responding to seemingly every police-related incident in the city.

The nights were long, too, as I found myself drinking too much, trying to unwind after another stressful day so I could turn off all the thoughts pinging through my head and get a few hours sleep.

Jack's death seemed to further my exhaustion. Then came the terrible morning of Sept. 11, 2001, when so many things changed forever.

Photos

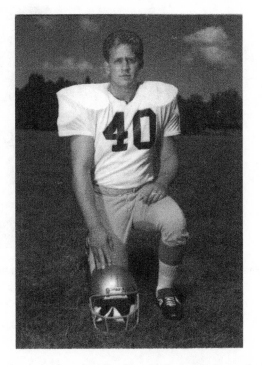

As a handsome, hard-working (and humble!) strong safety on the football team my freshman year at the University of Rochester in 1978. The truth was, I had more heart than talent for the game.

It shows Ed as the subject of a sports-in-motion photo shoot at the police academy.

Me and my proud father, Edward Norris, on the day of my graduation from the NYPD's Police Academy in January 1981. I couldn't wait to find out for myself what a cop's life was really like.

Dan Mullin (left), me and Jim LaPiedra on the roof of the NYPD's Mid-Town South precinct circa 1984. Both were great partners. I always knew I'd get home safely at the end of my tour when I was with them.

Yes, I was a mounted cop in the summer of 1984 in the Bronx. Yes, it could make a certain part of your anatomy sore. Training for the mounted patrol involved riding horses for eight hours a day for two straight months.

As a sergeant with the Brooklyn South narcotics unit. The anguished citizen to my right had just been arrested for selling heroin after we broke through his apartment door in the Red Hook neighborhood with a battering ram.

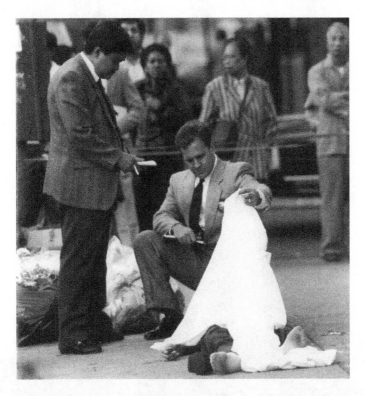

Investigating a Chinese gang murder on Manhattan's Lower East Side circa 1989. The deceased had tried to rob a gambling den at gunpoint – his last very bad idea.

Me pictured between NYPD commissioner Bill Bratton and dapper, bow-tied Jack Maple on the day I was promoted to captain in 1994. Bratton was a terrific leader who re-energized the department in the mid-90's; Maple was a life-long friend and mentor and godfather to my son, Jack.

Leaving the scene of a tense standoff with a serial killer who had barricaded himself in his Queens apartment in the late 1990's. That's Chief of the Department Lou Anemone, a long-time friend and mentor, to my left in the photo.

One of the happiest days of my life was the day I took my infant son Jack home from the hospital on June 15, 1999.

*Juggling a fidgety Jack after being sworn in as Baltimore police
commissioner May 9, 2000, as Kate and my mom looked on with delight.*

*Me standing in front of Baltimore Police Department headquarters circa
2001. Is that a great recruiting poster on the building or what?*

Mayor Martin O'Malley reading me the oath of office as I'm sworn in for my second term as Baltimore's police commissioner in 2002, with Kate and Jack looking on.

Me on patrol in a Baltimore alley in 2002. I went on patrol every day and made a point of wearing the same uniform as the street cops, not the dress uniform of the command staff.

Showing off a large cache of illegal drugs and guns found in a traffic stop on I-95. This photo was taken the day I was officially sworn in as State Police superintendant – I had raced up to Harford County earlier that morning to congratulate my troopers for the drug and gun haul and show my support.

Facing the media with Gov. Bob Ehrlich (left) and Lt. Gov. Michael Steele on the day of my official swearing-in as Maryland State Police Superintendent, March 14, 2003. I'm ashen-faced on what should have been one of the happiest days of my life – all the reporters wanted to talk about was the corruption indictment rumored to be coming down.

My prison ID card, which you were required to hold up whenever there was a body count inside the fence. I look mean enough to scare a snake, which was the whole idea. As a former police officer who feared retribution if his identity were known, I wanted to look like a hardened criminal when I went in.

I carried this photo of my son Jack every day of my incarceration, to remind me what I was fighting for.

In my new life as a radio talk show host, I was broadcasting from the site of the Fort Lauderdale Grand Prix in 2006. We were there because Baltimore also hoped to lure the prestigious auto race to its downtown.

Me with "The Wire" actors Michael Williams (left) , who played the notorious Omar, and Lance Reddick, who played Cedric Daniels.

*At a screening of "The Wire" in Manhattan with actors Bill Williams and
Jim True Frost. I got to walk the red carpet like a real actor!*

12

The Darkest Day Yet

A warm, sunny morning, four sleek passenger jets commandeered by terrorists roaring out of a crystalline blue sky to deliver death and destruction – who could have ever imagined such a thing?

I had gone to my office at police headquarters early that day. Like so many other Americans, I watched in horror as images of the Sept. 11 attacks were shown on TV: smoke billowing from the north tower of Manhattan's World Trade Center after the first airliner hit; the second jet plowing into the south tower and igniting a tremendous fireball moments later; the scenes of panic and devastation at the Pentagon outside Washington, D.C. after yet another airliner crashed there; the south tower collapsing in an unholy jumble of noise, rubble and dust; the fourth jetliner after the hijackers crashed it into a muddy field outside Shanksville, Pa., the north tower caving in as crowds of workers, residents and tourists fled in terror.

My hometown had been attacked. So had the nation's capital. Both would have a profound effect on my psyche. Yet in those anxious first hours, with America under siege and thousands of civilians and first-responders already killed, I had no time to put any of it in context.

I had to worry about protecting Baltimore.

Clearly, no one knew what was coming next. No one knew if other cities had been targeted, if this was simply the first wave of deadly attacks and others would follow in the days ahead.

Thankfully, we had prepared for something like this in Baltimore. Immediately, I cancelled all vacation time and time off in the department, and had every police officer in the city mobilized. We called public works and ordered them to fill every dump truck they had with sand, and to position them in front of all our sensitive locations to prevent car bomb attacks.

I was doing hourly press conferences the day of the attacks, trying to look strong before the TV cameras in order to keep everyone calm and assure them that we were ready for anything. Meanwhile, I was worried sick about my father and brother. Both worked near the World Trade Center, and with phone service out, I couldn't find out if they were safe or not.

It was not until the next day, when a couple of my NYPD buddies reached me, that I learned my dad and Robert were OK. By then, I was wearing combat fatigues, carrying an MP-5 submachine gun and patrolling Pratt Street at the Inner Harbor with other officers, marveling at the eerie stillness, with not a car in the streets or a person on the sidewalk. It was a surreal scene that would be repeated in dozens of cities all over the country.

For months after the deadliest attacks on U.S. soil in our nation's history, I would be consumed with survivor's guilt.

I'd lost a number of friends in the World Trade Center attacks. Most were cops and firemen. But two of my dearest friends who died were Danny Richards, a bomb squad detective and karate buddy, and John O'Neill, a former neighbor of mine and an ex-FBI agent who had chased Osama Bin Laden forever.

John had gotten a job as the head of security for the World Trade Center. On the day of the attacks, he had reportedly helped the FBI and the New York Fire Department set up a command center in the lobby of one of the towers while also helping bring people to safety. He was last seen walking toward the north tower when it collapsed.

Making my remorse even worse was my involvement with the

Meir Kahane case years before. The knowledge that we might have stopped future terrorist attacks by cracking down harder on Kahane's cohorts, and paying more attention to the intelligence gathered, would haunt me for a long time.

Still reeling from Sept. 11, the country faced a new threat exactly one week later: letters filled with deadly anthrax spores, mailed anonymously, began arriving at the offices of members of Congress and various media outlets.

Soon, the U.S. was in a full-blown panic. The letters seemed to be popping up in random cities. Over a dozen people suffered from anthrax inhalation. An employee of American Media in Florida died of anthrax poisoning in early October. Less than three weeks later, two postal workers in Washington, D.C., died of the same cause, as did an employee of the Manhattan Eye, Ear and Throat Hospital.

Again, no one knew what was coming next, whether the letters presaged other anthrax attacks in other locations. It was reported that the lethal microscopic spores could be placed in food and water, or released into the air from buildings and planes and trucks.

By this point, though, I was growing increasingly frustrated with federal authorities, feeling they were deliberately keeping local law enforcement agencies out of the loop on these attacks.

Whether it was to protect their sources – or whether they felt they were the only ones smart enough to handle the investigation – they were refusing to share information that I felt could help police departments all over the country protect their citizens.

Finally, on Sept. 25, the local FBI office agreed to hold a briefing for us about the 911 attacks. It took place at Maryland State Police headquarters in Pikesville. The briefing, however, turned out to be a complete charade. Essentially, we were told nothing more than what we'd been reading in the newspapers for days.

The FBI gave us a ho-hum Powerpoint presentation with grainy photos of the suspected hijackers, and little else of substance.

As the meeting wore on, I was getting more and more fed up.

Finally I could keep quiet no longer.

"What else do we have?" I snapped. "Do you even know for certain if these guys were actually on the planes? Have they been identified? Have their bodies been found? Any identifying remnants?"

The agent giving the briefing rolled her eyes.

"Well," she said, "their names were on the flight manifest."

"Yeah?" I said. "You think a terrorist might lie? Or travel under a false name?"

I was furious. Here we were, still shaken from these monstrous attacks, desperate for any nugget of info that might help us anticipate and prevent another one. And we were *still* getting jerked off by the feds.

Just then I got a message on my Blackberry.

"Oh, by the way," I told the assembled agents, "another letter with anthrax was just found at NBC News in New York. Apparently it was mailed to Tom Brokaw. The police are headed there now."

Unreal.

Here we were, not getting squat out of the feds. Yet here I was, giving *them* info on one of the biggest investigations in their long and storied history. Because of my lack of confidence in federal authorities, I had earlier contacted major police agencies on the East Coast and requested to have Baltimore detectives in their operations bureaus, and offered to host their guys in ours. New York and Washington, D.C., did it with us and it worked well. That's why, with our detectives on-site in Manhattan, I had been notified immediately of the latest anthrax threat.

Then early one morning in October, while I was at the Starbucks in Mount Washington fueling up for the long day ahead, I received a call from the FBI.

"We have information that at 1 o'clock this afternoon, there's going to be an anthrax attack in Baltimore," an agent said.

"Have any other cities been mentioned?" I asked.

"No," he said.

"How credible is the information?"

"Credible," was the terse reply.

OK, at least this was a start. At least the feds had given us *something*

No other American city had been mentioned. And the intel had come from a credible source. I didn't give a shit about who the source was. All I wanted was the information. This allowed me to meet with my intelligence people and figure out what we wanted to do.

Finally, a decision was made: we would hold a press conference to let the people of Baltimore know there had been a threat.

But we also decided not to evacuate the city. It was 10 in the morning, we were on full alert, and the folks we were charged to protect had been informed. I was comfortable with the steps we had taken.

One p.m. came and went and nothing happened. We breathed a sigh of relief. There was no attack. And nobody had missed work, nobody had been evacuated, nobody had panicked. With a little help from the feds, I was able to do my job, and I was grateful for that.

But my rift with the government agencies soon grew even larger. For one thing, word got back to me through a friend that the FBI was making fun of me.

"That fucking idiot," the Bureau people were saying, "he's happy with any information we give him. Doesn't even care where it comes from."

Which was true – in its own way.

As I tried to tell the feds: I don't give a shit if you overheard something in a coffee shop in Paris or you beat it out of somebody in Egypt. I don't care how you got it or who your source is. I just need the raw intelligence. After that, I'll make a decision if I think it's credible.

That's all police chiefs really needed to do their jobs. And the feds never got that point.

As the weeks went on, I kept voicing my frustrations. When the government began issuing color-coded terrorist alerts six months after the 911 attacks, I complained that the alerts made no sense, and were more confusing than enlightening.

FBI director Robert Mueller called when he heard about my latest criticisms.

"What's wrong *now*, Eddie?" he asked.

"What's wrong are these stupid alerts," I told him. "What do you want me to do? Do I look up? Do I look down? Where's the threat coming from? And what does it involve?

"Is it my water supply?" I went on. "Is it my infrastructure? Are there going to be guns in schoolyards? I gotta know what to look for!"

Mueller never seemed to have any answers. And neither did anyone else on the federal level.

In early October, Martin O'Malley and I were asked to testify before a subcommittee of the House Committee on Government Reform about our concerns that the feds were freezing out local police departments in the fight against terrorism.

Yet in the days leading up to our appearance before Congress, I was very worried about the repercussions of testifying.

I knew how the government could ruin your life if you took them on. But I had already briefed Maryland Senator Barbara Mikulski on the lack of cooperation we were receiving. And when Barry McCaffrey, the retired general and Vietnam War hero who had served as President Bill Clinton's drug czar, told me it was my duty as an American to testify, I did.

"We have to know what the FBI knows about threats, tips and even just rumors," I told the subcommittee. "Why aren't we all working together to find the people the FBI is looking for?"

At another point, I said: "The FBI has a total of 11,533 agents. There are nearly 650,000 local law enforcement officers in the country. We want to help, and I think the nation needs us to help."

(This was beautiful: when I called the FBI press office before my testimony to find out exactly how many agents they had, they refused to tell me. Instead, I had to Google it. And I found the answer in about 10 seconds.)

I also brought up the Meir Kahane case and talked about all the intelligence that had been unearthed and never pursued because various law enforcement agencies either ignored it or refused to cooperate with each other – and how both World Trade Center attacks might have been stymied if they had.

By all accounts, our frank remarks were well-received by the sub-committee. And our testimony became a huge media story all over the country.

"As we shudder at the certainty that more terrorists lurk among us, a former New York City cop has presented the U.S. Congress with the best and perhaps only effective strategy for preventing another attack," wrote columnist Michael Daly in the next day's *New York Daily News*. "The cop was Edward Norris, once NYPD deputy commissioner and now police commissioner of Baltimore."

I was glad that I'd unburdened myself on a matter that was so important – and that had so many implications for the welfare of the country.

But one thing was certain: the FBI was now rip-shit mad at me. And that was never a good thing for a police chief to have hanging over his head.

Soon enough, I'd wonder how much my candor about the feds had contributed to a campaign of whispers and lies swirling around me.

13

"Too Tony Soprano"

As the months went on, the grinding pressure began to wear me down. I was drinking even more now, not getting enough sleep, not exercising nearly enough.

Not only were we consumed with keeping the city safe from terrorists and the daily fight against crime, but our officers were being killed at an alarming rate. This only deepened my funk.

Officer Kevin McCarthy and Sgt. John Platt had been killed when their patrol car was broadsided by a drunk driver. Officer Kevon M. Gavin had died after a high-speed chase when a budding young hit man – wearing body armor and carrying a 10 mm semiautomatic handgun – plowed his car into the back of Gavin's cruiser and pushed it 100 feet down the street. Officer Michael J. Cowdery, Jr. had been on patrol in East Baltimore when he was fatally shot in an ambush.

(The most brutal killing of all would come months later, when Detective Thomas G. Newman, off-duty at the time, was ambushed and shot outside a bar by three assailants. After Newman died, a doctor in the operating room showed me the detective's heart.

(The sight shook me as few others had. The heart had four bullets sticking straight out of it. Which meant someone had stood directly over his fallen body to pump the last few shots that had ended his life.)

I was so fried after McCarthy and Platt were killed that I was already thinking of quitting the job and going into private industry

— anything to get away from the madness of Baltimore's killings and a police department seemingly beyond repair.

But a train ride to Manhattan quickly disabused me of the notion of leaving.

In my Amtrak car that day, sitting directly in front of me on opposite sides of the aisle, were two smug yuppie businessmen who apparently fancied themselves as towering captains of industry.

Each of these dickheads was carrying on a loud cell phone conversation with his office designed to let the rest of us know how important he was.

"I don't *want* a Cadillac," the first was overheard saying at one point. "I asked for a *Lincoln*."

The other seemed to be talking even more loudly to someone in New York, apparently berating that person for not being the next Al Roker.

"I need to know what the weather up there is right now!" we heard the man bark.

Dude, I thought, *we're in fucking Newark, N.J.! The weather's the same up there as it is here. Look out the fucking window!*

Listening to these two mopes put me in mind of the great line in Shakespeare's Henry V, or at least my paraphrased version: "I could not die in such a man's company."

And I vowed I wouldn't. King Henry V went on to rally the English army before the Battle of Agincourt. And I would go back to rallying my own troops for the battle to save Baltimore.

It was, I realized, still the most noble mission I could undertake.

But nothing about it was easy. As the year 2002 began, I found myself having problems with both Martin O'Malley and his staff.

One incident in particular seemed to begin the downward slide in our relationship. In late February, after a black woman was raped near a bus stop in the Northeastern District, the police department soon found itself engulfed in yet another controversy.

The suspect was described as black and male, around 20 years old. But the next night, Major Donald Healy, the district commander, issued a memo to his officers that read: "Every black male around this Bus Stop is to be stopped until subject is apprehended."

Obviously, it should never have been written that way. You don't stop *all* black men at any time after a crime has been committed. In this case, the only people who should have been stopped were those who fit the description of the rapist.

Knowing Healy as I did, I was sure he hadn't written the memo. I was sure someone had written it for him. Someone who didn't know what they were doing. Or someone who had it in for the white major and had found a way to embarrass him.

When Larry Young, host of a popular talk-radio show with a huge black listenership, got hold of the story a week later, it became a huge deal. Martin summoned me to his office to ask what I knew about it.

"I have no idea – this is the first I've heard of it," I told him. "But I'll find out."

Yet by the time I got back to my office, a three-minute walk, Healy had submitted his resignation. Word was that the mayor had told Sean Malone, his buddy and the police department's legal advisor, to tell Healy he had to retire.

Upon hearing this, I went thermonuclear.

Forcing Healy to quit was absolutely the wrong thing to do. For discipline to be effective, it has to be viewed as fair, even when it's unpopular. *Especially* when it's unpopular.

Had Major Healy made a mistake? Maybe. Had he been set up? Possibly. But we needed to learn more about what had happened before jumping to conclusions.

In the meantime, we needed to remember that Healy was a well-respected commander with a 29-year body of work, a cop's cop, a former SWAT commander and street guy who was still passionate about his job.

Why would you want to lose someone like that? Here I had just lost another terrific commander, John Bergbower. And now *this* was happening.

As so often happened back then, matters quickly got worse.

The mayor called me again. This time he told me the shit had hit the fan, and that he was now taking major heat from black leaders over the department's handling of Healey.

"What are they unhappy about?" I said. "He's already retired. You made him retire."

"They don't feel that's enough," Martin said. "Can you take his pension?"

What?!

I was so white-hot angry I could barely speak.

"Take his pension?" I said finally. "Really, they're not happy with just him losing his job? Hmm, I tell you what. Tell them this: I'm gonna drive down to his house, fuck his wife and burn the place down. Would that satisfy them?"

I slammed the phone down. As to how much my rant and biting wit ended up helping Major Healy, I never knew. But the bottom line was this: his pension remained untouched. And he was allowed to retire normally.

In the months to come, though, I'd have similar fights with the mayor and members of his administration. Martin was definitely not a cop-hater – he had started his career as a prosecutor, after all. But his inner circle was very anti-police.

At one point, Martin's closest advisors wanted to propose that if a police officer got sued, they would only indemnify the officer up to $200,000. This in a city where *everybody* sued, where the courts gave out million-dollar awards for a cop breaking a guy's pinkie.

"No, I'm not doing this," I said. "I'm not putting my cops in jeopardy like that. They'll never do *anything*. And I could be affected, too. I'm a sworn police officer in this state. What if I shoot somebody and get sued for $5 million and I'm covered for 200 grand? I'd be on the hook for $4.8 million! I'll resign before that happens."

Fighting all these battles grew more difficult when I began to hear that Martin's staff was badmouthing me to the mayor. They were telling him I was spending too much time in the gym, that our successes had gone to my head and I was doing whatever I wanted instead of focusing on our mission.

Soon, Martin was showing up unannounced at our ComStat meetings to check up on me, and summoning me to 8 a.m. staff meetings on Monday mornings. I wasn't stupid. No one calls early Monday morning meetings unless they want to send a message.

I began to hear that my popularity was starting to rankle him, too.

I was all over TV in those days, wearing dark shades and black leather jackets and pricey custom suits. At one point Martin told me I was "too Tony Soprano" and suggested I go buy some khakis at Joseph A. Bank. It was a fashion tip I summarily ignored.

One night as Martin and I were leaving the Owl Bar at the venerable Belvedere Hotel after a work meeting that included pints of Guinness, a group of guys at a nearby table spotted us.

"We love you . . .," they yelled, then after a dramatic pause, ". . . Commissioner!"

Martin turned on his heel and walked back to their table.

"What do you mean you love *him?*" he asked. "What about me?"

He seemed serious, and the guys at the table quickly replied: "Oh, we love you, too!"

After we left, Martin turned to me and said: "Nice job, Commissioner Bratton."

He was smiling, but not in a nice, friendly way. More like in a this-is-gonna-stay-in-my-hard-drive kind of smile.

The message was not lost on me.

Years earlier, when Bill Bratton had begun to outshine Rudy Giuliani – appearing on the cover of *Time* without New York's fiery mayor was a tactical mistake – Bratton's days as the city's top cop were numbered.

You never want to upstage your executive. So Martin's dig about Bratton was sobering. *Boy*, I thought, *I really gotta start being careful.*

Yet even though we were having unparalleled success against the bad guys – violent crime was down 14 percent that year alone and overall crime down 29 percent the past three years – Martin's most trusted confidantes continued to view me with suspicion.

My sense was that Sean Malone, deputy mayor Michael Enright and Matt Gallagher, the director of Baltimore's CitiStat program – the data-driven cousin of ComStat that tracked housing problems, trash pickup, snow removal, etc. – thought of themselves as the smart guys.

Me, on the other hand, they viewed as the out-of-towner, a little too rough, not very sophisticated, with an aggressive demeanor they found off-putting.

I was blunt and brash and pushed back when they tried to stick their hands in my department, which didn't win me any friends, either.

With my support from City Hall eroding, I began confiding in people like Lou Anemone and Bill Bratton.

Bratton came down from New York at one point and the two of us talked in my office.

"Eddie," he said, "I want you to look at everything I did with Rudy and do the complete opposite. You've got to learn to manage your boss."

But I was never very good at that, so Bill Bratton's advice mainly went in one ear and out the other.

To give Martin his due, not too many mayors would have put up with a police commissioner who was as in-your-face and plain-spoken as I was. Oh, I wasn't stupid about it. I would never embarrass him in front of others. But I always let him know what was on my mind.

At this point, it seemed almost too late to take Bill Bratton's advice. The gulf between me and the mayor and his advisors was growing ever wider.

It didn't help when, a few weeks later, I began appearing on what would become one of the most critically-acclaimed cable TV series of all time.

If Martin resented the attention I was getting now, this would probably make things even worse.

And that's exactly what it did.

14

"The Best Show Ever on American Television"

"The Wire," HBO's gritty crime drama set on the bleak and forgotten streets of Baltimore, first aired in the summer of 2002. The new show included the unlikeliest of cast members: a certain squat, hard-assed police commissioner who had never taken an acting lesson in his life.

Invited to appear in the series by the show's creator, David Simon, I made my dramatic debut in episode six in early July playing – stay with me here – a hard-bitten homicide detective named Ed Norris.

I know, I know . . . what a stretch, right?

Think about the acting chops needed to pull off such a role!

But my very first line surely hinted at the innate talent about to blossom before the cameras, and the truck-load of Emmys that would certainly come my way.

Walking away from the bloodied corpse of a kid who'd been tortured to death, Detective Ed Norris, lamenting how screwed up things are for a hard-working *poh-leece* like himself, snarls: "Show me the son of a bitch who can fix this department, and I'll give back half my overtime."

Oh, how the critics raved!

OK, actually, I'm not sure the episode was even reviewed, much less that my small role was mentioned. But David Zurawik, the Sun's television critic, *would* later write of my performances: ". . . He has a natural energy and raw anger that are in perfect sync with the dominant sensibility of the series."

(Raw anger? *Moi?* Hey, if that was the best compliment I could get, I'd take it.)

The series, of course, was not kind to Baltimore. This was no gauzy Chamber of Commerce documentary, complete with stirring soundtrack, about the renaissance of a great American city shedding its old blue-collar image in a joyful, head-long rush to embrace the New Millennium.

No, the first season of "The Wire" was all about the brutal drug trade terrorizing the city's worst neighborhoods and the hapless, resource-stressed and often incompetent police force trying to keep it at bay.

Naturally enough, Martin and many of Baltimore's mandarins were appalled to see their beloved Charm City portrayed in such a bleak and desperate light.

"I really don't need an HBO special to tell me what the problems of this city are," O'Malley told reporters. "I do not promote problems. I choose to address them."

But the depiction of Baltimore in "The Wire" was never going to be anything but honest and unsparing about the city's ills – at least those all but crippling its most neglected neighborhoods.

As best-selling horror novelist Stephen King would write: "In David Simon's version of Dante's Inferno, Hell is played by Baltimore and all seven of the deadly sins are doing just fine, thanks."

My involvement with the show began months earlier, when David asked me to lunch not long after I'd been named commissioner.

I knew who David was, having watched "Homicide," the great NBC crime drama of the 90's based on his book by the same name. In fact, I remembered watching it when I first came to Baltimore, looking at the new uniforms the cops wore and listening to their strange lingo and thinking: *I can't believe I'm in charge of a department that's being featured on a television show!*

At that lunch, David explained what "The Wire" was about and that he was just beginning to cast the show. He talked about how much he disliked my predecessor, Tom Frazier, whom he felt was a bumbling bureaucrat who had cluelessly dismantled a solid police department. It was Frazier's dysfunctional police force, David said, that was the inspiration for the new series.

David said he liked the job I'd been doing so far and felt the department was headed in the right direction. But he also made it clear that "The Wire" was going to be very critical of the fictional Baltimore police it depicted.

"The department's not too bad now – I've really tried to correct a lot of the problems," I replied. "The problem is, you guys never miss. HBO always knocks the ball out of the ballpark. So everyone is gonna see it and think nothing's changed. I wish you had picked the LAPD."

But he hadn't, so this was something I would have to live with.

"OK," I asked, "is the police commissioner in the series going to be a black guy or a woman?"

Nope, David said. A white guy.

"OK," I went on, "is it set in the past or the present?"

The present, he said.

"Great," I said, throwing up my hands. "Now *everyone's* going to think it's me."

Yet I wasn't really offended. This was TV. This was entertainment. I totally got it. And I felt the viewers of a sophisticated cable series tackling serious issues of drugs, poverty and urban blight would be enlightened enough to make that distinction, too.

The day after our lunch, a letter arrived for me at police head-quarters. It was from David Simon.

After thanking me for my time, he got down to business. Given our discussion, he wrote, would you be willing to appear in a cameo role in "The Wire" playing a detective who criticizes the commissioner?

In effect, he continued, you'd be criticizing yourself. And this would be an inside joke for Baltimoreans that would lessen any ill feelings about the department being cast in a harsh light.

He added that I would get paid – maybe not enough to buy a luxury yacht, but the Screen Actors Guild minimum. And I could save the money, invest it, squander it, give it to charity, or do whatever with it.

I was immediately intrigued. And when Martin signed off on the idea, I told David I was in.

So it was that a few months later, I found myself in a dreary alley in West Baltimore, shooting the scene where Detective Ed Norris studies the mutilated corpse of gay stickup artist Omar's boyfriend and grouses about his non-functioning police radio, the fact that no one has come to collect the body, and how fucked up the department is.

People asked if I was nervous during the filming of the scene, but I wasn't.

My feeling was that everyone already knew I wasn't a real actor, so how humiliating could it be if I screwed up? Plus it actually helped my confidence to know that I was the only one there who had actually *done* this stuff, raced to the scene of a homicide and stood over the stiffening corpse of yet another poor soul gunned down in the city's endless drug wars.

Still, doing the shoot was exciting. So was hanging out with actors like Dominic West and Wendell Pierce, who played Detective Jimmy McNulty and Detective Bunk Moreland, respectively. As I walked off the set that first day, David approached me.

"You know, you're not that bad!" he said. "Want to do it again?"

Sure, I said. And I did, appearing in a total of 22 episodes over five years.

From the very beginning, the reaction within the police department to the new show was mostly positive. Most people thought it was kind of fun having the commissioner appear in a series set in

Baltimore, no matter how dark and uncomfortable the subject matter could be.

The public seemed to like it, too – even when some of the things I was doing on-screen were less than savory.

In an episode titled "Dead Soldiers," Detective Norris comes staggering out of a bar as a Pogues tune is blaring from the jukebox and the police are holding a wake for one their dead comrades. Norris is holding two shots of whiskey for McNulty and Moreland, who are equally-hammered, with Bunk slumped wearily on the curb.

"Wake up and die right, you cunts!" Norris barks. And after giving them the shots, he proceeds to puke all over the street.

Oh, yeah, he was all class, that Detective Ed Norris. But years later, on my radio talk show, a caller would remember turning to his girlfriend after watching that scene and exclaiming: "That's our *police commissioner*! How cool is that?!"

Obviously, the spewing scene won't go down as one of the great dramatic moments in television history. But it was fascinating for a novice on the set to get an inside look at how it was filmed.

For one thing, they used 24 cups of tomato soup and corn chowder mixed together to create the fake vomit. They shot the scene from all angles and it required 24 takes. In half of them I was speaking, in the other half I was, um . . hurling.

When we finally finished shooting, Dominic West and Wendell Pierce started laughing, shooting me knowing looks that said: *C'mon, you're too good at this! You've clearly done this in real life!*

Another bit of "Wire" insider trivia: if you ever wondered why the characters didn't speak with that distinctive "Bawlmer" accent, the answer is simple – and hilarious at the same time.

David said they had originally tried having the characters on "Homicide" speak in vintage "Bawlmerese." But the feedback from the public had been almost entirely negative. Apparently viewers hadn't known whether they were supposed to laugh at many of the lines, because the characters using the accent sounded mentally-handicapped.

All in all, "The Wire" was great fun to do and it was an honor to be associated with such a brilliant and timely show.

Jacob Weisberg, writing in Slate, called it "the best show ever broadcast on American television." And Stephen King would add: ". . . its take on America's drug war makes 'Miami Vice' look like a Saturday morning cartoon."

Yet as critically-acclaimed as it was, it was hardly watched.

All sorts of theories were put forth for this discrepancy: its subject matter was too disturbing. It had an almost all-black cast, which might have turned off white viewers. Its multiple, inter-woven story-lines and lengthy list of characters were too hard to keep track of. A lot of people didn't have cable or HBO at the time.

Another mystery was how, year after year, a show as groundbreaking as "The Wire" would get shut out for television's top awards.

Not once was it nominated for Outstanding Drama Series, the Emmy's highest honor. And while it was nominated twice for Outstanding Writing for a Drama Series, it never won that, either.

"It's like them never giving a Nobel Prize to Tolstoy," Weisberg wrote in Slate. "It doesn't make Tolstoy look bad, it makes the Nobel Prize look bad."

In a lot of ways, I think TV people simply over-looked David Simon's talent, viewing him in much the same way that a lot of cops had viewed Jack Maple.

With Maple, a lot of cops thought: *The guy was a transit cop, not even a real police. He never even graduated from high school! He has an equivalency diploma! And he doesn't even look like a cop!*

With David, who started as a newspaper staffer for the *Baltimore Sun,* the TV mavens thought: *Who's this fucking baldheaded police reporter from Baltimore? He thinks he's going to break into this industry? Ha!*

As for me, I feel that I owe David in so many ways.

"The Wire" introduced me to so many smart, funny people that I would never have met on my own. People all over the country and in Europe still recognize me from the show, too, which is good not just for my ego, but maybe for any future TV or documentary work.

David's belief in me never wavered. Neither did his support. And just one month after "The Wire" first aired, when my world would begin to crumble – slowly at first and then with astonishing speed – I'd need all the support I could get.

15

The First Rumblings of Trouble

On a warm summer day in 2002, Ragina Averella, the police department's director of communications, came to me with an unusual request.

She said that Del Wilber, a reporter with the *Baltimore Sun*, had heard about something called the commissioner's supplemental account. He wanted to look at our records to learn more about it.

"What do you want to do?" she asked.

"Let him look," I said.

This was in keeping with my policy to be as open and transparent as possible. Unless what the media asked for involved an ongoing investigation or a matter where a crime victim or witness could be jeopardized, my policy was: Give 'em what they want.

I did the same thing here. I had nothing to hide.

"Ed understood the press," Ragina would tell a reporter years later. "He didn't view them as the enemy, as so many bosses do in law enforcement and the private sector."

When Wilbur made his request, all I told Ragina was to make sure he was supervised, and that he didn't take anything out of the building.

Then I forgot about the matter.

What's that old saying about no good deed going unpunished? Sure enough, for his kindness and munificence toward the media,

Commissioner Open and Transparent promptly got whacked upside the head.

On August 13, the *Sun* ran a front-page story with the bombastic headline: "Norris, police spend off-the-books funds on trips, gifts, meals."

The lead paragraph didn't get any cheerier:

"Baltimore Police Commissioner Edward T. Norris has used a loosely-monitored, off-the-books departmental fund to finance more than $178,000 in expenses during the past two years, including trips to New York, gifts to fellow officers and others, and expensive meals at trendy restaurants."

The article went on to detail a number of the expenditures, among them: sweatshirts and jackets I'd bought to keep police commanders warm at a chilly Orioles game. Cheap replica cufflinks I'd given as souvenirs to first-time visitors to Baltimore. Trips I'd taken to New York and other cities, including hotel and restaurant bills. A Palm Pilot I'd bought for work. A Glock pistol I had tested. Holsters I'd bought for my aides. Gifts for members of my staff. Hotel accommodations for out-of-town experts we'd brought to Baltimore to help with our departmental training.

Many receipts, the article said, were missing. Others failed to identify where the expenditure took place.

"I wish better records had been kept," I was quoted as saying. "I thought somebody would be writing this stuff down."

The department's budget and fiscal people had done a poor job of monitoring the fund. But ultimately, I acknowledged: "The buck stops with me."

Martin told the *Sun* he hadn't known about the supplemental account.

"I'm a bit angry there wasn't better and tighter accounting," he was quoted as saying. But he added that he stood behind me and that I was a "terrific police officer and terrific commissioner."

Even when the story broke, though, I still didn't think it was a big deal.

The commissioner's supplemental account had been around since the Great Depression, started as a relief fund for orphans and widows and gradually morphing into a discretionary fund to be used by Baltimore police commissioners.

Apparently, its existence had been little-known outside the department. But I had been briefed on it my first day as commissioner and told that it involved no taxpayer money and was not subject to city review or auditing.

"You can do whatever you want with it," I was told. "It's to be used completely at your discretion."

I saw that my predecessor, Tom Frazier, had refurbished a classic police car for the police museum with money from the fund. He had also bought a tuxedo for a formal function and spent $6,000 on lunches for his staff with fund revenue.

But even after that initial briefing about the fund, I pressed for more clarification on using the fund.

"If I want to buy a thousand dollars worth of bubblegum tomorrow, it's OK?" I asked.

"It's your money," was the answer. "You want to buy bubblegum, it's OK."

Nevertheless, soon after becoming commissioner, I tightened the parameters for the fund's use. From now on, any spending would have to be directly related to furthering the mission of the police department.

After that, though, I had never given the fund a second thought. Never looked into how it operated. Never paid attention to how much money was spent. But after the *Sun* story broke, the media – along with the city comptroller and City Council members – started beating me up about it.

Martin announced that he would turn over control of the fund to the city Finance Department and would hire the accounting firm of Ernst & Young to do an independent audit to investigate the spending.

I told the press I welcomed the move. And I did.

I had done nothing wrong. All of the expenditures under my watch had been for police business.

Yes, the supervision of the account had been shoddy. So had the record-keeping. But consumed as I had been with the never-ending task of trying to make Baltimore safer, it was something that had flown completely under my radar.

Years later, people would ask me: How could you not know what was going on with this fund?

And my answer was: "C'mon! I'm the CEO of a company with 3,200 people under him. The budget was $275 million. I would buy 50 or 60 police cars at a time! I didn't go out and count them. I don't go and check on how much gas is delivered to the precincts.

"It's just preposterous to ask an executive to do that. What executive checks on every single expense incurred on his watch?"

Ultimately, the audit would confirm that most of the roughly $180,000 spent in my three years as commissioner went for legitimate department expenses. Some $20,000 was flagged, mainly because of the lack of receipts and shoddy book-keeping.

But entertaining staff members at Orioles games, handing out cheap trinkets, replica police shields and other items as souvenirs for visiting dignitaries, buying restaurant meals for law enforcement experts in town to help train our department, buying items such as a Palm Pilot for work – all were legitimate expenses that a big-city police commissioner could reasonably be expected to incur.

(Ultimately, after resigning as commissioner, I would pay back some $7,500 in personal expenses rather than fight an endlessly dragged-out accounting battle. And Peggy Watson, the city's finance director, would confide the payback was strictly for show, to make it look as if I hadn't simply received a slap on the wrist for my transgressions.)

For a while, the stories accusing me of misusing the fund went away. A month later, I appeared at a press conference with Thomas

DiBiagio, the U.S. Attorney for Maryland, to announce a drug seizure from a joint operation between the city and the feds.

A *Sun* reporter asked DiBiagio if his office would be looking into the controversy over the police commissioner's supplemental account. DiBiagio said no. Maybe he would have spent the money differently, he told reporters. But since no taxpayer money was involved, there was no need for any investigation.

To my mind, the whole thing was now a dead issue.

But the events of the past year – the never-ending battle to make Baltimore safer, the Sept. 11 attacks and the new concerns about terrorism gripping our cities, the constant drumbeat of negativity from the press over the controversial fund – had definitely taken their toll on me.

I was exhausted, working ridiculous hours and hardly sleeping most nights before going back to work at two or three in the morning.

I began looking around for other jobs, police commissioner posts that were opening up in other cities as well as private consultancy jobs in New York. Big outfits such as American Express, Saloman Brothers and the New York Stock Exchange were always tapping former New York Police Department execs for lucrative positions heading up in-house security operations.

Why couldn't Eddie Norris get in on a gig like that?

Are you kidding? A chance to make a whole lot more money with far fewer headaches? Who wouldn't leap at that?

"It's a good time to leave," my old NYPD buddy John Miller advised. "You could dry-clean yourself of all this stupid fund bullshit. You did a good job in Baltimore. Now you move forward."

Nevertheless, I still had an obligation to the citizens of Baltimore, and I was determined to be the best police commissioner I could for as long as I held the job. But my stress levels were red-lining. I was getting dangerously burned out.

Then came the incident that permanently soured my relations with Martin and led indirectly to my swift departure as the city's top cop.

In November of 2002, I attended the election night party of Maryland's new Republican governor, Robert L. Ehrlich.

I had been invited by Lt. Nick Paros, who headed the union that represented some 1700 state police officers and commanders. Not long after I arrived at the downtown hotel where the celebration was held, the TV cameras zeroed in on me.

Looking back on it now, going there was a dumb move on my part.

I was naïve, and didn't realize how much my boss, a life-long Democrat, hated Ehrlich. Not only that, but I was avowedly apolitical in those days. In my mind, I was a cop and I ran a police department, period. Any decisions I made about whom to associate with were never based on politics or political aspirations.

But none of that mattered in this case. The shit hit the fan immediately.

Martin O'Malley appeared in my office first thing the next morning. To say he was unhappy is putting it mildly. When he gets pissed, his eyes get squinty, like Jack Palance in those old Westerns, when he's getting ready to grab one of the bad guys by the throat.

Martin said I had made him look bad by showing up at the party. Now, he said, he was getting a ton of calls from people essentially asking: what the hell was Norris doing consorting with the enemy?

The conversation with Martin was brief. I didn't fight him on this one. I said "OK, you're right" and I apologized. But a good deal of damage had been done.

Immediately, rumors began swirling that my showing up at Ehrlich's victory gala meant I was about to take the top job with the Maryland State Police. This was patently untrue – there had been no offer on their part and no lobbying on my part to join the agency.

Nevertheless, Martin asked me to go on-camera with Jon Leiberman, a reporter for WBFF-TV in Baltimore, to say I wasn't leaving and dispel the rumors. Dutifully, I did this.

Yet only a few weeks later, I received a call from Gary McLhinney, the former head of the Baltimore police union, who was now part of Bob Ehrlich's transition team.

McLhinney said the governor wanted to invite me to lunch at Harry Browne's Restaurant in Annapolis, the upscale, art-deco dining spot favored by many of the state's movers and shakers.

"He wants to talk about what the state police can do for the city," McLhinney said.

The lunch turned out to be an altogether pleasant affair. The governor made it clear that as a former kid from Arbutus, a Baltimore suburb, the city was important to him.

"I'm not going to forget about the city," Ehrlich told me, "because as the city goes, the state goes. We have to make sure Baltimore continues in the right direction. What can I do to help?"

I laid out a plan that called for state troopers to actually patrol in the city, and to have them do interdiction on highways to help us with drug trafficking, terrorism threats and every other kind of criminal activity.

At the end of our lunch, the governor dropped a bombshell.

"Would you be interested in that job?" he asked. "Running the state police?"

I was stunned. I hadn't seen that coming at all. But, hell, yes, I was interested! I was looking to leave the Baltimore PD anyway. I'd had three very tough years when we had accomplished a lot, but I was just like a peeled nerve at this point.

Heading the state police was like my dream job at this juncture of my career. I had never done that kind of policing, so it was a fresh challenge and a chance to work in the entire state with a very squared-away police agency.

Now I had a chance to get away from the stress and ugly racial politics of policing in Baltimore and still do the job I love. I wouldn't even have to move. I was living in the Mount Washington neighborhood of Baltimore and the drive to state police headquarters in nearby

Pikesville would take 15 minutes at the most.

Another reason to consider the state job was Ehrlich's interest in having me focus on terrorism. Since my testimony in front of Congress following the Sept. 11 attacks, I had become a national figure as someone who had taken the lead on this issue.

Whatever the terrorists were going to bring to hurt people, I told the governor, whether it was bombs, bullets or whatever, they would have to drive it somewhere. And the state police were the people to stop them, because they patrolled the highways.

"I'm definitely interested in the job," I told the governor. "But I've got to talk to the mayor first."

"No, we'll *both* talk to him," Ehrlich said. "I want to assure him we're not going to forget the city. This is going to benefit the city. You running the state police, you're obviously going to take care of Baltimore. And *I* want to take care of Baltimore. So we'll work together."

The next time I could see Martin, a day or two later, I told him all about my lunch meeting with the governor and the unexpected job offer.

"I really want to take it," I said.

Martin was not pleased – another vast understatement. I don't remember if his eyes squinted. I don't remember if he flashed the full Jack Palance death glare.

But he was mad as holy hell at me – *again.*

"If you're going to take a do-nothing job," he grumbled, "can't you do it in another state? Want me to call the governor of New Jersey? I'll see what I can do for you there."

But within minutes, he seemed to accept the inevitable. He got Ehrlich on the phone and we had a three-way conversation.

In a calmer and more playful tone now, the mayor told Ehrlich: "You're stealing my guy." But the governor attempted to paint the move in a rosier hue. Everything would be OK, he kept insisting. Eddie's taking the state police job would be a win-win for both the city and state.

So it was that on New Year's Eve, I made a recorded announcement over the Baltimore police radio, informing the rank-and-file that I was leaving as police commissioner and taking a new job as state police superintendent. I also assured them I was not leaving Baltimore, and I thanked them for all their hard work.

Predictably, the media pummeled me once news of my new job leaked out.

The spin now was: Commissioner Ed Norris is abandoning the city. He came here and talked tough about being the man to help transform Baltimore. But now he was cutting and running.

At a news conference in Pikesville, I was peppered for a half-hour with questions about my motivation for switching jobs and my state of mind, the inference being that I was making a terrible mistake because of cloudy judgment.

"Why would you leave the city?" Terrie Snyder, a reporter for City Paper, asked somewhat incredulously.

"Well, I always looked good in earth tones," I replied.

It was a flippant answer and probably not the best way to endear myself to reporters who might now be covering me in my new role. But by this point, I had had enough of the media piling-on and didn't care.

Not long after, a package was delivered to my house in Mount Washington. It turned out to be a farewell gift from Martin: a beautiful framed photo of General Ulysses S. Grant.

This had been an inside joke between us.

When times were good and crime in Baltimore had decreased, the mayor would address me as Gen. Grant, after the victorious Civil War hero. But when the violence and drug wars spiked, I became Gen. George B. McClellan, the indecisive and ineffective Union commander eventually replaced by President Abraham Lincoln.

On the back of the photo, Martin wrote: "Congratulations on your new job. Thank you for all your work. You saved a lot of lives in Baltimore. Sincerely, Martin."

I was touched by the kind gesture, and the photo would soon grace the walls of my new office at State Police headquarters.

As 2003 began, I was pumped up about my new job, grateful for a fresh start in the business of keeping the citizens of Maryland safe.

Unfortunately, the mood would not last very long. Another shitstorm was lurking just over the horizon, one that would blow in and upend the world of Col. Edward T. Norris, the proud new superintendent of the Maryland State Police.

16

"What Are They Looking For?"

Just a few weeks into the new job, I was attending a police funeral in Snow Hill on Maryland's Eastern Shore when I got a call from Ragina Averella at Baltimore police headquarters.

"I hate to tell you this," she began, "but some people from the U.S. Attorney's office just came by. They're removing all the records of the supplemental fund."

My heart immediately sank.

That's the downside of being in law enforcement and knowing how federal prosecutors work – how the sausage is made, if you will. From the moment I took Ragina's call, I knew, almost intuitively, my career would be over. Because once the feds get interested in something, they never let it go.

Ask yourself this: do they ever come up empty-handed? Have you ever seen a press conference where federal prosecutors announce: "We found nothing, sorry for wasting your time?"

No. Never. They'll find *something*. If you cheat on your taxes, if you leaned on your mailbox as a kid or cherry-bombed it or whatever – they'll find some stupid law you've violated. And owing to a bullshit statute known as U.S. Code 666, they can come in and investigate any entity – such as a police department – that accepts $10,000 in grant money from the federal government.

I went back to the funeral service with my mind racing.

I've been hounded and hounded and hounded since the day I came to Baltimore, I thought. *I'm a fascist, I'm a Nazi, I'm a racist – it never ends. Now they're still chasing me. Why can't I just live a normal life?*

Why can't I just be sad at a funeral like everyone else? Instead, I gotta have this fucking atomic bomb dropped on me . . .

News of the federal investigation was leaked to the media with shocking swiftness. On February 28th, the *Sun* ran another front-page story headlined: "Grand jury probes spending by Norris from city fund."

While I didn't comment directly that day, Major Greg Shipley, the state police spokesman, relayed to the newspaper that I felt the issue was "old news" and that my use of the commissioner's supplemental fund had been thoroughly investigated.

But from that point on, life for me became a nightmare.

The steady drip-drip-drip of leaks to the media seemed to occur on a daily basis. The investigation was all anyone wanted to talk about. Rumors of possible indictments were already out there.

My official swearing-in ceremony as the new state police superintendent took place in Pikesville on March 14. It was a beautiful, sunny day. My family was there with me and so were many of my old police friends from New York. In the audience were bigwigs from the FBI, Secret Service, U.S. Marshals Service and other law enforcement agencies.

It was supposed to be a joyous occasion. But the photos from that day tell a different story. Flanked on stage by Governor Bob Ehrlich and Lieutenant Governor Michael Steele, I looked stiff and ashen-faced, a shell of myself.

Naturally, in the press conference after the ceremony, all anyone wanted to talk about was the investigation. I'm not sure there was even one question about the state police.

Over and over, the reporters asked a variation on the same theme: "What are the feds looking for?"

And over and over, I gave the same answer: "I have no idea. The last person they're going to tell is me."

The presser turned into this brutal interrogation that went on and on. In the videos that made that night's newscasts, you can see me almost visibly recoiling with each new query.

Obviously, it was hardly the ideal way to begin a new career. Bill Bratton had told me that the first year taking over an agency was the most fun.

"You get to put your people in place," he said. "You get to make your big changes and put your stamp on the agency."

But this was anything but fun.

This was the Department of Justice's version of the Spanish Inquisition, only with English sub-titles.

In the weeks that followed, I learned that many of the people connected to me – friends, relatives, members of my inner circle when I was Baltimore police commissioner – were being subpoenaed and yanked in front of the grand jury.

I tried to focus on the agency, but each new rumor about the investigation had me whipsawing between hope and despair.

"This is all going away," friends would say. "It's all bullshit. They've got nothing."

But just when I'd start to believe them, I'd hear from someone else: "Jesus, they just brought the manager of the Smith & Wollensky steakhouse in to testify."

Meanwhile, my attorney, Andy Graham, was having zero luck getting any information about the investigation from the U.S. Attorney's office.

"This is absolutely Kafkaesque," he would tell me. "They won't tell me what they're looking at. They won't tell me how long it's going to go on. I have no idea what we're doing here."

And this was a guy who had been an assistant U.S. Attorney!

Despite this metaphorical axe now swinging over my head, there were times I could lose myself in my new job and feel almost a sense of normalcy.

One day when I was on patrol near the Maryland-Delaware border, acting on a tip from an informant, John Miller, my old NYPD buddy called.

"How're you holding up?" he asked.

"Couldn't be happier," was my reply. "I'm sitting in a state police car in the median strip of I-95, waiting for a carload of guns to come across the state line. So I'm in heaven."

There were even precious moments of comic relief that I so badly needed. One occurred the day Steve Chaney, chief of operations, and I visited the state police barracks in McHenry, the western-most station before the West Virginia line.

As the new superintendent, I had set out to visit every barracks in the state, mainly to shake hands and introduce myself, but also to keep everyone on their toes. On this visit, Steve and I happened to drop in at the ungodly hour of 4 a.m., both of us dressed in full uniform.

A trooper sat at a desk watching TV. He had his tie off and his feet propped up, the picture of relaxation.

"Hey, how are you?" he greeted us casually.

"Good, good," I said.

"Quiet night," he said.

The two of us continued chatting for a moment. Then I saw him glance at the wall behind me, which contained the official head-shot photos of Gov. Ehrlich, Lt. Gov. Michael Steele and me. The trooper's eyes went from me to my photo a couple more times.

Suddenly he spotted the twin silver eagles affixed to my collar. And with that, he shot to his feet, stood ramrod straight and yelled: "JESUS CHRIST!"

"Relax," I said, as Steve and I burst out laughing.

"*Nobody* ever comes out here!" the poor guy wailed, provoking more laughter.

But as the weeks went by and the investigation dragged on, I became more and more depressed. Now rumors started circulating that the federal prosecutors were looking into women I might have fooled around with.

The feds had questioned John Miller about who I had brought to my NYPD retirement dinner in New York, after I had already started work in Baltimore. They wanted to know whether it was my wife who had accompanied me.

What kind of question is that regarding a federal money case? I wondered. Miller had wondered aloud about the same thing when he was grilled by the feds.

"Oh, this isn't the Ken Starr investigation," one had told him, alluding to the former Whitewater independent counsel who looked into President Bill Clinton's sexual transgressions. "We're just asking."

Just asking. Right. Sure they were.

By August, the *Sun* was reporting that members of my security detail from my police commissioner days had been subpoenaed to testify, which seemed to fan even more conflicting rumors.

"OK, I hear they're announcing Friday that they're dropping the investigation," a friend with connections to the U.S. Attorney's office told me.

But the next day the story had changed.

"I hear the indictment's coming down Tuesday," another friend reported.

Meanwhile I was fielding daily calls from the media and meeting with high-powered lawyers – one was Fred Fielding, former White House Counsel for Presidents Ronald Reagan and George Bush – who assured me I probably wouldn't go to prison if indicted, but would probably lose my job.

I was holding my breath the whole time, going through my workday in a leaden funk, trying to keep my family calm and drinking myself into a stupor every night, just to be able to sleep.

One day, after I ran a meeting with the gun lobby regarding which firearms in the state were to be regulated, it all caught up to me.

When the meeting was over, I stood up, smiled and shook

everyone's hand. Then I went in my office, closed the door and my knees buckled. I literally collapsed in my chair, my head spinning and my breath coming in quick, shallow gasps.

How much longer can I do this? I wondered, staring blankly at the ceiling.

But there was no answer up there, either.

17

The Eight-Point Buck
Goes Down

On a hot day in August, I came home from work to find my wife, Kate, waiting at the foot of the stairs.

She wore a concerned look – well, an even *more* concerned look than the one she usually wore now.

"Let's sit down for a minute," she said. "I have some news."

I groaned and slumped against the banister. By this point, just about everything was freaking me out. I could tell this would be yet another sunny bulletin that neither of us wanted to hear.

Kate said that my parents had called. Federal investigator had shown up at their house in Brooklyn that day and served them with subpoenas to testify about a mortgage application letter, as well as a check found in my bank records.

That's it, I told myself. *They got me. I know exactly what they're going to do with this.*

The thing I had worried about for months was now staring me in the face. Two years earlier, when I had bought my house in Mount Washington, I had borrowed $9,000 for closing costs from my father.

We had both signed a letter saying the nine thou was a gift. But when I paid my father back, the transaction had technically become a loan. Which meant I had lied on a mortgage application, a federal offense.

Sure, it was the wrong thing to do. But just about everybody I knew did this gift-loan maneuver with their folks. And the reason was simple: we did it because we were poor. Because nobody had any money. So you borrowed off your parents. But who the hell ever gets prosecuted for it?

Actually I knew the answer to that from my work with the Department of Investigation in the NYPD.

Back then, we had done a lot of prosecutions with the feds. And if you had a suspect you were targeting and couldn't get him for, say, extortion or murder, there were all sorts of other violations – many of them tax-related – that could put him away.

Now that the tactic was being used on me, I was even more terrified of being indicted.

In a private moment with Gov. Ehrlich, not long after my folks had been questioned, I had moaned about the feds: "Why are they doing this to me?"

"'Cause you're the eight-point buck in the state," the governor replied. "Who else are they going to do it to?"

If that was true, the eight-point buck was now squarely in their sights. And they were just itching to pull the trigger.

A couple of months later, while with another trooper on a car-stop on I-95, I got a call from the manager of the Coach store where I had shopped for luggage. She said the feds had called her in to testify and asked her a series of weird, sexually-related questions, including if I had ever taken nude photos of her.

It was so bizarre to think that the U.S. government would be asking citizens these kinds of questions in a financial case. Even if they thought the woman was one of my girlfriends, wouldn't they be asking her whether I had ever taken her on vacations? Or lavished her with gifts?

I was so shaken by her call I almost passed out on the highway.

What the fuck are these guys up to? I kept asking myself.

But that night, as I stood in the shower, I had an epiphany.

Suddenly I started punching the shower walls and screaming at the top of my lungs: "MOTHERFUCKER! MOTHERFUCKER! NOW I GET IT! NOW I KNOW WHAT THEY'RE DOING!"

Thank God my wife and son were on a trip to California, or Kate would have called an ambulance to take me away.

But now it hit me: there wasn't enough with the supplemental fund business for the feds to hang me. Now they had added the whiff of sex. Now they were going to smear me with allegations about my infidelities and use the charge of mortgage fraud as their trump card – a charge that carried a maximum sentence of 30 years.

"Yeah, that's the headshot," attorney Fred Fielding would soon confirm. "They're going to pepper the indictment with things you didn't do. They're going to indict you for bank fraud and mortgage fraud. And they're going to force a plea because they have you on that."

As soon as Kate returned from California, I told her: "I'm done. And there's nothing I can do about it."

At this point, I was so dispirited that I thought about suicide, going so far as to sit in Robert E. Lee Park one day with my gun. Only the thought of my son Jack living without a father kept me from pulling the trigger.

One thing was certain: I wanted to be mobile when the indictments came down. So we put our house up for sale that fall, sold it immediately and moved into the apartments at Harborview downtown.

In early December, I went to Gov. Ehrlich with every intention of resigning. I was still running the state police, going to meetings and dealing with the media, but the pressure of the looming indictment was killing me.

At times, I thought I was going to have a stroke. Day after day, it seemed, the government was leaking allegations that made me look more and more terrible. And the fact that I couldn't defend myself was driving me crazy.

"No, we're going to fight this," Ehrlich said when I tried to quit. He said he still didn't actually believe I'd be charged.

But two days later, on Dec. 10, 2003, as I drove to the Starbucks in Mount Washington to meet my wife, a call from my lawyer made it official. An indictment was being handed up that day.

When I met Kathryn outside of the coffee shop, she was all smiles – until she got a good look at me. I had tears in my eyes as I told her what had happened. And I resigned as superintendent of the Maryland State Police that day.

The sweeping indictment announced by Maryland U.S. Attorney Thomas M. DiBiagio charged me with using the Baltimore Police Department's supplemental fund to pay for personal expenses, including gifts, private travel and liaisons with girlfriends. My former chief of staff, John Stendrini, was also indicted for misapplying police money and obstructing justice by lying to city officials about how the money was spent.

Yet as I studied a copy of the indictment with Kate the night before I was to surrender to a federal magistrate, my hopes were buoyed.

"This is all bullshit," I said as we leafed through the pages. "This is nothing. It's petty stuff and it isn't true, and we'll fight this."

To my mind, this was all a regurgitation of the stuff the city had investigated months earlier.

Personal expenses? The $242 spent on custom-made shirts were *police* uniform shirts, made because I wear a size 50 jacket with an 18-inch neck. With a build like that – like a standup freezer – it was tough to buy clothes off the rack if I wanted to look professional.

The $163 for boots bought at Dan Bros. Discount Shoes? Those were combat boots I bought the day after the Sept. 11 attacks, so I'd have something to tuck my combat fatigues into while on patrol. A $200 knife had actually been a police rescue knife, which we used to cut seat belts out of cars.

On and on it went. Candles? There had been a power failure in my neighborhood and my security detail had brought them to our house. Kate had offered to pay for them, but had been waved off. Same with liquor I'd had delivered to my house. I had offered to pay for that, too, only to be told: "No problem, Commissioner. It's been taken care of."

The pricey restaurant meals and hotel bills they wanted to kill me on were bogus, too.

A $376 meal at Flemings I supposedly had with a girlfriend to celebrate her birthday? I had actually been with a member of the police department and two other men. Bar bills and food bills in Toronto were for my staff when we attended a police chiefs' conference after the Sept. 11 attacks. Trips to New York had all been for legitimate police business, as well as for the wake and funeral of John Stendrini's mother.

Sure enough, though, the last page of the indictment charged me with making a false statement on a mortgage application.

OK, I thought, *they have me on that one. And that could be serious, 'cause they have my father as a co-conspirator. But the rest of it? A joke!*

If you're wondering how Kate reacted to seeing romantic liaisons with other women listed on the document, she was pretty much numb to it by this point.

She had heard the whispers and rumors of my infidelities for months, and had been hurt deeply by them. The truth is, I had lied to her and denied any wrong-doing, trying to protect her from even more pain now that her husband was under siege and her entire world was being turned upside down.

I'm certainly not proud of betraying her. This is no excuse, but the stress of running a big-city police department, the heavy drinking and the number of women who routinely threw themselves at cops – including the new commissioner – created the perfect environment for an affair. And I was too weak to resist it.

Walking into a Canton bar late one night, I heard two women call my name. When I looked over, they smiled, pulled up their T-shirts and flashed me. And that was hardly the first time women let me know they were available.

But spare me your moralizing on the subject of infidelity, please. As recently as September of 2016, the Journal of Marital and Family Therapy reports that 57 percent of men and 54 percent of women admit cheating in a relationship. The bottom line is that this is a common and very personal issue between a man and a woman. The fucking federal government has no business in your bedroom.

But here's the bottom line: I never spent a dime from the fund on these women. Allegations that I bought train tickets from the fund for women to visit me in New York, that I wined and dined them in restaurants and bought gifts for them from Victoria's Secret – none of it was true. (And there's this: when the feds were figuring out my so-called restitution for all these alleged gifts to women, it came to a grand total of $100.)

Yes, I had met other women for a glass of wine or dinner on my trips to Manhattan. But these were *work* trips for the Baltimore PD. Unlike what was alleged, I didn't travel there for the purpose of having trysts.

Understand, even though I felt the government's case was weak as I perused the indictment, I was still terrified.

Believe me, seeing "the United States of America vs. Edward T. Norris" at the top of the page was a sobering sight. This is a country that topples governments! We run the world! And now that chilling phrase was saying, in effect, that I was taking on the legal might – and had incurred the wrath of – the most powerful nation on earth.

Andy Graham and a new, experienced defense attorney, David B. Irwin, recommended by Governor Ehrlich, accompanied me for my hearing before the federal magistrate. (Another heavy hitter, Joseph Murtha, had also joined our legal team. Yes, the same Joe Murtha who had defended Linda Tripp on state wire-tapping charges for her role in the Monica Lewinsky scandal that led to President Bill Clinton's impeachment.)

The prosecutors played hardball from the beginning: they wanted my passport taken and my guns surrendered immediately. But my lawyers emphasized that I was hardly a flight risk – what was I going to do? Take off and leave my family? As for my weapons, they reminded the judge that I had put a lot of people behind bars in Maryland and still had security concerns.

After pleading not guilty, I was allowed to keep both my passport and firearms and was released on my own recognizance. In a brief meeting with the media afterward, I said I very much looked forward to my day in court.

Flashing a thumbs-up sign, I mustered a smile and answered a reporter's shouted question of "How are you doing?" with a simple "Fine." Then, trailed by a platoon of TV camera crews and still photographers, I left the courthouse, seemingly the very picture of confidence.

Of course, it was a complete façade. Inside, I felt totally dead. It was a wonder my brain could even function, and that my rubbery legs could still keep me upright.

"We're going to attack the indictment both on the law and its constitutionality," Andy Graham told the media afterward. "And we're going to attack the facts because many of the facts are just plain wrong.

"You will hear in the final analysis that all these expenditures were appropriate and appropriately related to police business," Andy added.

But I knew leaving that courthouse that my life would never again be the same.

My next move was to get out of Dodge – to move my family somewhere far from the madness that had swirled around us all these months.

Now it was getting scary for us in Baltimore. The day after the indictments were handed down, Kathryn happened to be driving downtown. When she had stopped her car at an intersection, a man selling newspapers had lunged at her, holding up the front page of the *Sun* with a photo of me and the headline: "Chief Lies, Cheats, Steals."

Those had been the stinging words DiBiagio had used to describe my actions to reporters. Later, I'd learn the words would cause him to be hit with an ethics violation, because it made it harder for me to get a fair trial. But now the headline was being thrown in my wife's face by some nutcase running up to her in traffic. No, we were getting the hell out of this town --that much was certain.

"Being at the bottom of the abyss is like hitting the lottery in the sense that you're now free," I told Kate. "Now I have nothing. So we don't have to stay here. The good news is: we can go anywhere we want and start from scratch."

We settled on Tampa, Florida, where I had a friend, Debbie Kurtz, who had worked as a consultant to Rudy Giuliani. My plan was to work with her for Giuliani, who had been hired by the Mexican government to overhaul the notoriously corrupt federal police, or *federales*.

My thinking was this: *Ok, the feds have gotten me to resign. They've humiliated me publicly. But there's no freaking way they're going to move forward with this bullshit case.*

In my more optimistic moments, I assumed I'd be hit with kind of federal misdemeanor charge that would keep me out of law enforcement, but still allow me to carry a firearm and do consulting or security work for private or quasi-governmental agencies.

Luckily, I was still working as an actor on "The Wire." David Simon continued to be incredibly generous toward me. OK, I wasn't getting Brad Pitt money, but I was getting the SAG minimum, which helped. And David was paying for my flights to and from Baltimore, as well as for my hotel stays.

That's how I spent the next few months as we geared up for the trial date, which had yet to be announced. I would try to stay busy, work on the set of "The Wire," do things around our townhouse, go to the beach, listen to music. But the whole time Kathryn and I were worried sick about what lay ahead.

As time went on, I was even more amped up to fight the charges. But my attorneys had been negotiating with the federal prosecutors, both sides trying to see if we could avoid a trial. And ultimately, my legal team convinced me that the best thing to do was take a plea deal.

For one thing, they said, it would cost somewhere in the neighborhood of $500,000 to hire private investigators, forensic accountants and other experts needed to mount a successful defense. Secondly, the feds had assured my lawyers that they were fully prepared to hammer me on the mortgage fraud charge.

"If he doesn't take a plea," one prosecutor said, "he'll never see his son grow up."

My 71-year-old father was also being threatened with jail on the mortgage fraud charge. And the whole ordeal was already taking a considerable toll on him.

After sitting in on one meeting with my lawyers, during which we were told that the *Sun's* negative editorials about me were likely to sway the judge into treating me harshly during a trial, my dad erupted.

On the way home, he began punching the steering wheel of the car and screaming: "THE *BALTIMORE SUN'S* GOING TO INFLUENCE WHETHER YOU GO TO PRISON OR NOT? I CAN'T BELIEVE THIS!"

So it was that on March 8, 2004, I appeared once again in U.S. District Court in Baltimore and pleaded guilty to conspiring to misuse money from the Baltimore police commissioner's supplemental fund and lying on tax returns. In return, the charge of lying on a mortgage loan application would be dropped at sentencing.

That was an awful day for me.

Standing stone-faced in front of the judge, with my hands clasped in front of me, I balked when asked if every word of the indictment was true. (I'd soon learn this was a standard question in such proceedings.)

"I'm not saying that!" I hissed to my attorney, David Irwin. "That's bullshit! It's not true!"

But Irwin squeezed my hand and whispered: "Calm down. You're pleading to a conspiracy to misuse this fund. All they have to do is have one charge be true and you're guilty of the entire conspiracy."

Unbelievable. In other words, if they could prove that I'd done one thing wrong – accepted the candles without paying for them, for instance – I'd be found guilty of the entire conspiracy. Where in God's name is the justice in that?

Addressing the media after I left the courthouse, Irwin said: "He made the decision that a long drawn-out trial would bring too much pain to his family, his friends and the city of Baltimore. Now he'll try to pick up the pieces with his family and put this behind him."

The only good thing – if you could call it that – was this: according to my attorneys, prosecutors were saying they would not recommend jail time. It seemed the worst they would hit me with would be house arrest and probation.

Still, a felony conviction – it was clear prosecutors would accept nothing less – would kill me in other ways. My life depended on my ability to carry a gun and work in law enforcement. No one in that field would hire me now.

Yet at age 44, I was still a relatively young man. I still had many years ahead of in the work force. And now I'd have to start all over again.

After the guilty plea, I went back to BWI airport right away. Waiting for my flight to Tampa, I sat forlornly at the bar, sipping a Manhattan.

When I tried to pay, the bartender shook her head.

"No," she said softly, "when you were here, my street was safe."

When you're as down as I was, you take your little kindnesses wherever you can get them. This was one I would never forget.

Kate and I flew up to Baltimore for my sentencing, and the sentencing of John Stendrini, on June 21, which would prove to be another terrible day. My mother and father drove down from New York to be with me. Standing in front of the packed courtroom, with a huge media throng, I felt my life was over.

John was sentenced first. He received three years probation and was ordered to pay a hefty fine and perform 300 hours of community service. Then it was my turn to face the judge, and now there was a stirring in the room.

John had been the warm-up act for this ugly little farce. But I was the one everyone had come to see.

"This courtroom has seen a vice-president, this courtroom has seen a governor, and now it sees a police commissioner . . .," Judge Richard D. Bennett began, alluding to the infamous corruption trials of Spiro T. Agnew and former Maryland governor Marvin Mandel in the 70's.

At this point, he droned on about the importance of integrity, which was ironic. As a ranking state Republican, Bennett had helped Thomas DiBiagio get the U.S. Attorney job, which meant the judge should have clearly recused himself from the proceedings in the first place. It was just further evidence of how corrupt the whole thing was.

As Bennett continued talking, my father suddenly bolted from the courtroom in tears, in the throes of a massive anxiety attack.

"I knew right then what was going to happen," he would say later.

Sadly, so did I – as much as I hoped I was wrong.

"Eddie is a great father and I need him with me at home, to keep our family together," Kate pleaded to the judge. But it wasn't looking good.

When it was my time to speak, the tears were flowing freely.

"I fully accept responsibility for what happened here," I said. "I know what it's done to the police department. I know what it's done to my family. I said I was sorry for this many, many times. I'll be saying it for the rest of my life."

But ultimately, none of what was said had any effect. Neither did the letters of support from Maryland government officials, and from Rudy Giuliani and Howard Safir, that my lawyers submitted.

"If there was ever a time in the history of this country that we need to depend on the integrity of the police, that time is now," Judge Bennett intoned, referring to the shaky mood of the nation in the wake of the Sept. 11 attacks. "This was the wrong time for two outstanding cops to make a mistake."

When he finally read the sentence, it hit me like a blow to head: six months in federal prison. Six months of home detention after that. A fine of $10,000 and restitution of $12,000 (even though I had no money left from the expense of trying to defend myself.) And 500 hours of community service – 100 hours over the recommended maximum sentence.

Judge Bennett said he would recommend that I serve my time at the minimum-security federal prison at Eglin Air Force Base in the Florida Panhandle. But he said the final decision on where I would go was up to the Federal Bureau of Prisons.

I had 30 days to turn myself in.

And with that, the hearing was over.

Kate and I were devastated. I remember being escorted from the courtroom in a daze and the media mob engulfing me. They were like animals, pushing and climbing over each other to get at me with their microphones.

"WHAT DO YOU SAY TO THE PEOPLE WHO SAY YOU GOT OFF TOO EASY?" someone shouted over the howling din.

But I was through talking. There was nothing left to say – to them or anyone else.

On the flight back to Tampa that day, I don't think Kate and I said a word to each other. We were both too wrapped up in our own gloom, and the terror of not knowing what lay ahead.

When we arrived back at the townhouse, we were greeted by Kate's parents, who had flown in to watch Jack for us while we traveled to Baltimore.

"How did the sentencing go?" they asked as we walked through the door.

"It couldn't have gone any worse," I said.

With that, I went up to our bedroom and closed the door. And I didn't come out for a long time.

18
Preparing for the Unthinkable

I spent the first few days back in Florida in an almost catatonic state.

For hours on end, I would hole up in the little office in my townhouse, brooding about all the ways my life had gone off the rails and second-guessing myself up for all that had happened.

Should I have watched the supplemental fund more closely? Should I have asked to see the books every day?

All those times I asked for the check at a restaurant, only to be told by a staff member "Don't worry about it, Commissioner" – should I have followed up to see how it was paid?

When I'd mentioned that I wanted to stock up on liquor at the house and a detective had appeared at the house with a case of wine or booze, should I have pushed some cash on him even after he said: "It's all taken care of, sir?"

In the days after the sentencing, I must have gone through the indictment a hundred times, trying to remember every trip I took, who I was with, why we went and what we spent. When I wasn't doing that, I was on the computer, researching everything I could about life in a federal prison.

The prison at Eglin Force Base was nicknamed "Club Fed" for the supposedly easy time inmates served there. But that didn't exactly have me breaking out the champagne and party hats.

For one thing, there was no guarantee that I'd be sent to Eglin. Secondly, as a former police officer – and a high-profile, big-city police *commissioner* – I would not be arriving as just any other prisoner.

Ex-cops have a notoriously tough time in prison, with any number of inmates eager to exact revenge on a member of the hated fraternity that put them behind bars. With that in mind, I hired a personal trainer to help me get in the best shape possible. All the eating and drinking I'd done to alleviate the stress of the last few months had taken their toll. I needed to get down to fighting weight – literally – once again.

Dealing with people was stressing me out, too. Whether it was at the gym or at a restaurant or a bar, I would invariably run into some insensitive asshole that had heard about my upcoming sentence and felt compelled to remind me of the horrors I might face.

"Oh, man, prison! That's gotta be terrible," one guy said to me. "Aren't you afraid of getting raped?"

Gee, the thought never occurred to me, I wanted to say. *But thanks for bringing it up. That makes me feel a lot better.*

I saw a psychiatrist for anti-anxiety meds and went into hyper husband-father mode to at least keep the family intact.

To keep life normal while I was gone – or at least as normal as possible – I sold my nice Volvo, gave the money to Kate and told her to use it for a down payment on a house.

There was no question that the entire ordeal was stressing my marriage big-time. I was a basket case and incredibly hard to live with. Even though I had cheated on her, I still loved Kate deeply. And she had been really strong the whole time, when a lot of women would have fallen apart.

Think about all she was dealing with: income gone, husband going to prison, a child who still needed to be raised with love and attention. And now she was living in yet another strange city thousands of miles from any family.

In another attempt at normalization, I also bought 26 little toys for Jack, along with the same number of cards and envelopes, which I filled out and addressed. Jack was five at the time, and the plan was that Kate would give him a toy each week and tell him Daddy had mailed them.

But the thought of leaving him soon was breaking my heart.

One night, as we sat watching a Spiderman animated movie on TV, Jack suddenly pointed at the screen and asked: "Why is Spiderman in jail?"

Say what?!

I had been lost in my usual morose thoughts, barely paying attention. But now I snapped out of it.

What's that?! Spiderman's in the slammer?

What do you say to a kid when he hits you with that one? With why a revered comic-book super-hero is suddenly shown slumped dejectedly behind bars?

"Well," I said, picking up on the story line, "sometimes bad people put good people in jail, Jack."

Yes, the irony was rich here. I had said this just to plant that tiny thought, that chip, in Jack's brain. Someday, I knew, we'd sit down and talk about everything that had happened to me while he was growing up. That's when I'd try to make him understand that the real dangerous people in this world don't always carry guns.

Sometimes they wear suits and ties and frozen smiles.

As crazy as it sounds, I also took to sleeping on the tile floor in my son's bathroom during this time. It was another way to be close to him in the days I had left at home. But I also wanted to get used to sleeping on hard, shitty surfaces, in case the accommodations in prison were as horrible as some had said.

Even when I wasn't obsessing about how depressing my life was now, I couldn't entirely escape it.

One day I went to lunch at a Bar Louie restaurant with my friend Debbie Kurtz. One of the TV's nearby was tuned to CNN. Seconds later I watched incredulously as a crawl at the bottom of the screen flashed by: "Former Maryland State Police Superintendent Edward T. Norris is scheduled to turn himself in soon to begin a six-month . . ."

"I can't fucking believe this!" I said. "I'm that interesting? I'm a national news story? Really?"

A week or so before my reporting date, the government made it official: I was to be incarcerated at Federal Prison Camp, Eglin in Fort Walton Beach, Florida. I didn't want my father or my wife to drive me; the long drive from Tampa would have been too hard on them, and way too emotional for all of us.

Instead, a couple of my old buddies from the NYPD, Rick Burnham and Joe Martinez, offered to fly down and drive me. They rented an SUV and we set out on the morning of July 20, the day before I was scheduled to turn myself in. The plan was to drive to someplace close to the prison and spend the night there, and then I'd report to the facility the next day.

Saying good-bye to my wife and son that morning tore me up inside. I tried to appear strong, smiling at Kate and telling her not to worry, that I'd be back soon and life would get going for us again. I hugged and kissed Jack and told him I had to go on a trip for work, but I'd be sending him something special in the mail each week.

I gave a jaunty wave and walked out. But as soon as the door closed behind me, I began to sob uncontrollably. The next thing I knew, I was doubled over, my whole body heaving as if I were having a convulsion. Thankfully, Rick and Joe made believe that they couldn't see me, giving me a moment's privacy and sparing me from feeling even more embarrassed.

We talked as we drove, but it was awkward for all three of us. They felt terrible for me, a good friend who had also been their boss and their leaders for years. Now, of course, I was relying on them to prop me up emotionally on this horrible journey.

In some ways, though, the trip came to resemble "The Last Detail," the bittersweet Jack Nicholson movie of the 70's. That was the one about two Navy men ordered to bring a young sailor to prison, only they decide to show the kid a good time on the way.

In a way, that's what happened on this trip. We checked into a motel near Eglin, had dinner at a steakhouse and then hit a strip club and an Irish bar as the long night devolved into a boozy blur of wine, bourbon and Manhattans.

Yet I was up early after a fitful few hours of sleep. Brutally hung over, I started banging on the doors of my buddies' rooms screaming: "Wake up! Wake up! Let's get this done! The quicker I get there, the quicker I get out!"

As Rick and Joe got themselves ready, I went back to my room and made a couple of calls to say good-bye.

The first was to Kate, who became so upset she had to put the phone down. We didn't talk long. The second was to Jayne Miller, the veteran investigative reporter for WBAL-TV in Baltimore and one of the few media people I trusted to get my story right.

"I'm checking into prison now," I told her. "You know I didn't do this, right?"

"Yeah, I know, babe," Jayne said in her gravelly voice, her words oddly comforting.

After that we drove over to the prison camp, on the sprawling Air Force base in Eglin, where we ended up at the wrong gate.

"Stay there," a voice on the intercom said. "A prison van will come pick you up."

People always want to know what was going through my head in the moments before surrendering my freedom. I was scared, sure. Afraid for my safety, of course. And I was sad to be leaving my wife and kid.

But the most powerful emotion I felt was basically no emotion at all.

I felt dead inside, like my soul had died. No joy, no hope, just . . . nothing.

When the prison van came to pick me up, Rick and Joe remained in the SUV and stared mournfully at me.

"Just fucking leave! I shouted. "I'm serious! Direct order! Don't look at me! You're just making this worse!"

Finally, the two drove away. Later, they would tell me they were so upset that they didn't say a word to each other for over an hour.

I climbed into the van and we drove slowly to the prison's processing center, where I got my first look at the place that would be my home for the next six months. Wearing a T-shirt, jeans and lace-up logger boots, I walked in carrying a bible and nothing else.

The bible was a gift from the Catholic priests at St. Jude Shrine in Baltimore. I am not a religious person, but I *am* spiritual. St. Jude, I knew, was the patron saint of lost causes.

As the doors clanged shut behind me, I wondered if I'd be calling upon him soon.

19

Locked Up

One of the first things they make you do upon reporting to federal prison is fill out a ton of paperwork, almost as if you're buying a car or applying for a mortgage.

They ask you the usual stuff: date of birth, Social Security number, occupation, etc. But from there the questions quickly get darker and more pointed.

They ask about any gang affiliations. They ask about any martial arts in which you're proficient. They ask about any tattoos you have. They ask about any training you had in the military.

Are you an expert in weapons? Explosives? Hand-to-hand combat?

And that's when it hits you: you're not filling out all these forms to buy a Hyundai Sonata. Or a nice Cape Cod on a quiet cul-de-sac somewhere.

No, you, my friend, are going to prison. And the hard-eyed people running it want to know just how much trouble you're capable of causing while you're their guest.

If there was any lingering doubt about your new life, it quickly disappears when they take your clothes and shoes and make you change into a snappy outfit of khaki shirt, khaki pants and slip-on sneakers. An ID tag is affixed to your shirt with your name and prison number. (Mine was 41115-037, which I'll remember for the rest of my life.)

Then they give you a bedroll and hand you over to a doctor for a cursory physical exam. Naturally, with my luck, the doc turned out to be a dick to the 10th power.

"What health issues are you concerned about?" he asked.

"Well," I said, "I'm having problems with anxiety."

"In prison, you're *supposed* to be anxious," he said.

Thanks, Doc. That's very helpful. Yes, very helpful indeed.

"OK, what else is on your mind?" he continued.

"Well, my weight has spiked," I said.

"OK, then stop eating," he said.

Right. Nice talking to you, Doc. It's been an absolute pleasure.

To my great relief, once I was escorted into the yard, the prison looked more like a college campus than the Big House. There were no fences, no razor wire. Instead, what you saw were a series of low-slung buildings and walkways bordered by grass and palm trees.

It wasn't exactly Club Fed – there weren't any marimba bands playing and bikini-clad waitresses serving frozen cocktails. But it sure didn't look like the photos I'd seen of Attica, either.

Inmates were hanging out everywhere, all of them checking out the new guy as I was led to my building. Instead of prison cells, Eglin featured an open-dormitory setting. Each building housed a couple hundred inmates, with bunk beds everywhere, similar to what you'd see in a military barracks.

When I finally reached my bed, a few of the prisoners came over and introduced themselves. One was a big old guy they called Goat Head.

Finally I asked him: "Why do they call you Goat Head? Your head's not that big."

He explained that when he first arrived at Eglin, they were hurrying him through the processing phase. To speed things along, this one red-neck guard with a thick Southern accent kept shouting what sounded like: "Go 'haid! Go 'haid!"

"Sir, why are you calling me Goat Head?" the confused newcomer asked. But somehow, the nickname stuck.

The other inmates began asking me where I was from and what I did on the outside. I had grown a mustache and beard and shaved my head to disguise myself as best I could. At first I told them I was a government consultant, which would have been partially true if I had landed a job working for Rudy Giuliani.

Hearing this, a thin, dark-haired man said: "Hey, can I talk to you for a second?"

When we were safely out of earshot, he said: "First of all, relax. There's not a lot of violence here. It's pretty laid back for a prison. Second of all, everybody knows who you are. We get newspapers, we watch TV. So we've been waiting for you to get here."

Oh. Hearing this, I chuckled to myself. *Guess I wasn't as slick as I thought.* Then I walked back inside and told them who I really was.

"Look, I know everyone in here is innocent," I said. "But I *really* am." And then I went into my whole sad story and how the feds had managed to put me behind bars for what essentially was a shitty little $9,000 loan.

The thin, dark-haired prisoner who had advised me to come clean would turn out to be Martin L. Grass, the former CEO of Rite Aid, who was serving an eight-year term for conspiring to inflate the value of his company.

But it turned out – big surprise! – that I wasn't the only one in there who'd been screwed over for patently unjust or obscure reasons.

One kid was doing federal time because he'd been busted for marijuana possession while driving through Fort Bragg, N.C. If he'd been popped anywhere outside of a military base, he would have gotten a slap on the wrist at worst. Another guy from Tennessee was in there for "misprision of felony" a little-known "crime" that involves knowing a felony has been committed and not reporting it to the police.

Eglin, I would learn, was mainly populated with drug offenders. Only 20 percent of the inmates had been convicted of so-called "white collar" crimes. The rest were people who had been caught up, in one form or another, in the drug trade.

But there could be no crime of violence in their past, which was one of the reasons disputes among the inmate population rarely rose above the level of occasional fistfights. To avoid those, there was plenty to keep the prisoners occupied: basketball courts, a soccer field used mainly by the Latino prisoners, a weight room, TV room and chapel.

There was even plenty of sex available if you wanted it. My new inmate pals showed me a sandy stretch of ground called Pinga Beach that abutted an inlet. Pinga, they noted helpfully, meant penis in Spanish. And Pinga Beach is where you could go at night to get a blowjob from prostitute prisoners, if you were so inclined.

As a new prisoner, I was assigned a job on a work crew cutting grass with a weed-whacker. Which was when I came face-to-face – literally – with my first dickhead cracker guard.

He was intent on being a hard-ass, laying down the law to a group of us newcomers to Federal Prison Camp, Eglin. In an icy, menacing voice right out of "Cool Hand Luke" or "The Shawshank Redemption," he began: "This isn't Club Fed anymore. There are rules here."

Suddenly he took a step forward, got right in my face and started screaming: "WE DON'T GIVE A SHIT WHERE YOU CAME FROM! WE DON'T GIVE A SHIT WHERE YOU'VE BEEN! THINGS ARE DIFFERENT HERE! WE RUN THIS PLACE, UNDERSTAND?"

When the rant was finally over and he walked away, I turned to another inmate and asked: ""What was *that* all about?"

The inmate shrugged. "He saw that Murder One haircut of yours," he explained.

Great. Apparently my shaved head made the guard think I was some bad-ass who'd been transferred from a hard-core prison to do my final bit at Eglin, where I'd surely attempt to have my way with everything.

As it turned out, though, the guard was a dick to everyone, not just me. Later that day, as our work crew sweltered under the broiling

Florida sun, he kept singing out: "NUTHIN' MAKES ME HAPPIER THAN SEEING GROWN MEN CUT GRASS IN 107-DEGREE WEATHER!"

When I wasn't working, I would often just lay in my bed with a stocking cap pulled low over my face and headphones on, listening to the radio. A lot of the inmates did this. There is very little privacy in prison, and this was a way to isolate yourself from your surroundings.

You didn't want to see what was going on, you didn't want to hear what was going on. You'd just sit there alone with your thoughts, brooding about how far you'd fallen, all the mistakes you made, all the people who'd screwed you over, how much you missed your family and what you planned to do with your godawful life when you got out.

Another way to lose yourself in prison was to read. During my six months behind bars, I would read 70 books. I read Tom Wolfe, Michael Crichton, everything Dan Brown wrote, including "The DaVinci Code."

I read the entire "Lonesome Dove" series by Larry McMurtry. I read philosophy books, obscure works of Russian literature like "The Master and Margarita" and anything else I could get my hands on.

Soon I fell in with a group of guys who would meet every day to smoke cigars and bullshit. One was Tyrone Marks, a drug dealer from New Orleans, who was about my age. He was well-respected in the prison camp and I was happy to befriend him, because if you were OK with him, you were left alone.

Another in the group was Dan Levitan, an investment banker from Fort Lauderdale. He was also an excellent chef who ran the prison kitchen. Soon, he asked me to come work there with him and watch his back, because disputes often flared up.

As I was to learn, the kitchen was the hub around which so much of prison commerce revolved. Inmates would steal things like fried chicken, steaks, peanut butter and potato chips and sell them for cash, drugs, cigarettes or anything else.

No wonder the guards searched you when you left the kitchen, although a lot of stuff still managed to walk out the door. The kitchen was like our own little stock exchange in terms of how many financial transactions it generated.

Another way to acquire things was to do jobs for others. Someone would do your laundry and you'd pay him in whatever the going currency was. At Eglin, it was cans of mackerel. Don't ask me why. I never saw anyone actually eat from the cans. But guys would have the cans stacked up by their bunks – that was their currency.

If you wanted your laundry done, for instance, it would cost you two cans of mackerel. A haircut, on the other hand, would cost you cigarettes. Why? 'Cause that's what the barber wanted instead of mackerel. Maybe he was sick to death of mackerel. That I don't know.

I'm telling you: banks could learn from these places. It was a beautiful system. Nobody's debts ever went unpaid, either.

Despite daily access to all that food, however, I actually lost 40 pounds fairly quickly. I'd walk for miles every day with my cigar smoker friends. I also had Kate send me the Weight Watcher's points book and I'd log everything I ate, sticking with lots of protein and vegetables.

Ironically enough, Eglin was also the most polite place you could ever imagine. People held doors for each other. They said "Good morning" and "How are you?" when they passed on the walkways.

They did this because everyone was angry and somewhat dangerous in their own way. Everyone was operating on a really short fuse. And no one wanted to be the guy who disrespected someone with some stupid slight and ignited an incident that could have easily been prevented with common courtesy.

Yet despite this veneer of politeness, you never forgot where you were. Even a minimum-security camp like Eglin had its prison rituals. One mandated that you knocked twice on the table before getting up after a meal, the traditional signal that you weren't rising suddenly to stick a knife in someone.

Again, this wasn't "Escape From Alcatraz." But it wasn't "Hogan's Heroes, either." Life at Eglin wasn't brutally harsh. But it wasn't a cake-walk, either.

The central fact of your existence was this: you had no freedom. All you had were people telling you what to do, when to go to bed, when to wake up, what to wear, where to work, etc. You were given 300 minutes on the prison telephone each month, which works out to about 10 per day, if you were good. If you weren't, sorry, no phone privileges.

All calls were monitored, too. And when the recipient of your call first answered, the first thing they heard was this cheery message: "This call is being made at the United States Penitentiary, Eglin . . ."

On the other hand, I must have been the only inmate at Eglin who hadn't somehow smuggled in a cell phone. At night, after lights out at 10 p.m., you'd seen the glow of cell phones winking on under blankets all over the room.

But God help you if you ever got caught with a cell phone. In prison, it was like having a gun. The penalty was severe, because inmates could order hits on their rivals and continue to run their criminal enterprises with a contraband cell phone.

Eventually, unless you were the most pissed-off, rebellious inmate in the whole world, you settled into the mind-numbing routine of prison life. You were up early because breakfast was served early – I'd be up at 5:30 every morning because chow was at 6. Then you headed off to your job for the rest of the day.

A really weird part of life in prison is that inmates are counted all the time. At certain times of the day, you were required to stand by your bunk or work place and be counted, which was supposed to ensure that no one had escaped. (A 4 p.m. count, I was told, takes place at nearly every prison in the country.)

It was a de-humanizing and demeaning ritual. But like everything else, you eventually got used to it.

I had been at Eglin a little less than two months when we were suddenly ordered to appear in the cafeteria at 5 p.m. that day.

"Bring your toothbrush and a book," we were told, "and nothing else."

The explanation turned out to be this: two hurricanes had already hit the Panhandle, causing varying degrees of damage. And now, with another powerful storm in Hurricane Ivan on the way, we were being evacuated to another prison, although the exact location was still hush-hush for security reasons.

We were loaded onto buses and we drove for many hours, eventually passing through flatlands with cotton fields as far as the eye could see. Only then were we told our destination: Yazoo City, Mississippi and a new medium-security prison that was actually still under construction.

This would turn out to be a fresh hell of unparalleled dimensions.

For one thing, when we finally arrived at the prison, we discovered there were no beds. No kitchen facilities. No phones. No nothing. Construction workers were actually still on site. It was a giant, half-finished concrete slab, for all intents and purposes.

We were told to pair up and find a cell. Tyrone Marks and I found one on the first floor, and that would turn out to be our new home for the next month or so.

Later that night, two huge box trucks filled with mattresses and bedrolls rumbled up to the prison. This set off a frenzied scene right out of "Lord of the Flies" as hundreds of wild-eyed inmates, under the harsh glare of the prison spotlights, fought each other to get a mattress before the supply ran out.

The prison would prove to be an absolutely miserable place. It made Eglin look like the Ritz Carlton. The cells were unbearably hot and humid and infested with the biggest black bugs any of us had ever seen.

Even though our cells were unlocked during the day, the prison was run like a maximum-security facility. There was razor wire everywhere. We were confined to our cellblock "pods" 23 hours a day and allowed to exercise in the yard for an hour. Also, the prison practiced "controlled movements," meaning prisoners could not walk around freely and were escorted to other areas of the facility only at designated times.

Since there were no phones, there were no phone privileges. This meant our families didn't even know where we were or what had happened to us in the wake of the powerful hurricane that had just roared through the Florida Panhandle.

Eventually we were allowed to call our loved ones and mail began trickling in. But by this time, word came down that we were about to be moved again. The Yazoo prison was simply not ready to adequately house inmates for any length of time without triggering a full-scale riot.

Lists were quickly posted with each prisoner's name and the new facility to which he'd be transferred. The news for me was not good: I was bound for the satellite prison camp at the U.S. Penitentiary, Atlanta.

The word was that Atlanta was a horrible place, an aging facility ringed by razor wire in the middle of the city, with a long history of violence.

Terrific, I told myself. *The ol' Eddie Norris luck is still going strong.*

20

Welcome to the Hole

The bus ride to Atlanta seemed endless as we wound our way through the red-clay fields of Mississippi, dropped a load of prisoners off at the Talladega federal prison in Alabama and continued on into Georgia.

There were 22 of us left on the bus, including a group of my original friends from Eglin, as we rolled on. I grew more and more apprehensive the closer we got to the city.

"Man, there are a lot of bad people in this place we're going to," I said at one point to Dan Levitan. "What if they find out I was a cop?"

Dan nodded thoughtfully. Then he stood and addressed the rest of the guys.

"Listen," he said, "when we get to Atlanta, nobody gives up Eddie's occupation. Everybody got that? It's important."

It was a wonderful gesture. To this day, I get teary-eyed just thinking about it.

People have all these pre-formed opinions of the men and women who are incarcerated. Sure, our prisons are filled with dangerous scumbags who would stab you in the back and take your money in a heartbeat. But there are lots of good people in there, too, good people who made a mistake – or two or three – and are paying for it, sometimes for the rest of their lives.

Anyway, the bottom line was this: I would be imprisoned in

Atlanta for three long months, three of the longest months of my life. Yet during those three months, not one of the 22 men on that bus would breathe a word about me being a cop.

Which is amazing. I can't imagine 22 people from *any* walk of life – police officers, radio talk show hosts, plumbers, lawyers, you name it – keeping a secret for that long.

The U.S. Penitentiary, Atlanta was a medium-security facility with high gray walls, forbidding guard towers and a shadowy glow that made it look like a castle out of a Frankenstein movie.

The satellite prison camp for minimum-security prisoners was next door. But as the bus inched its way down the narrow entrance ramp and the gates swung shut behind us, it was clear that we'd be spending at least the first night in the Big House itself.

It was well after dark when we arrived. We were strip-searched, given new (and horribly mismatched) prison clothes and photographed. Once again, whole forests had been destroyed for the amount of paperwork we were required to fill out during processing.

The kitchen was closed, so we were given Lunchables, the pre-packaged meals of meats, cheeses and crackers busy parents pack for their kids' school lunches. Standing in line with my newly-issued pillow and blanket, I looked down at the picture of Spiderman on the Lunchables box and almost burst into tears.

Lunchables, you see, were what I used to pack for Jack every day for school. But this was definitely not the time for anyone to see me all weepy. Because moments later we were led into the disciplinary segregation unit – the infamous Atlanta "Hole" – and confronted with a scene right out of a San Quentin riot documentary.

As we walked through a narrow corridor, inmates on both sides of us began banging on their cell doors and screaming through the food ports: "GET OUT OF HERE, YOU MOTHERFUCKERS! WE DON'T WANT YOU IN HERE!"

Dan had gone through this before, during an earlier stretch of his incarceration. Amid the horrible clanging din and the shouted oaths, he nodded knowingly at me.

"That's why I didn't tell you earlier what this place is like," he said. "I couldn't really describe it. And I didn't want to freak you out."

It turned out that the prison was already so over-crowded that the last thing these wild-eyed cons in the "Hole" wanted were more bodies crammed into their cells. Which was exactly what was happening: five or six inmates were now being shoe-horned into cells, leading to the altogether pleasant prospect of guys sleeping next to toilets and under sinks.

I was lucky – I ended up in a cell with only two other prisoners, who regarded me warily from their bunk beds. This will surely shock you, but neither of these large, heavily-tattooed gentlemen jumped up to give me a warm handshake or a welcoming hug.

After I exchanged muttered greetings and threw my blanket and pillow on the floor, they tossed me what turned out to be a tube of rolled-up newspaper wrapped in tape.

"Hold that roll under the door with your feet," one said. "It'll keep the rats out."

Rats?!

We gotta deal with rats now?

With that, the two turned away from me. Seconds later, the soft glow of a meth pipe illuminated the cell and two were taking hits off it and blowing the smoke into a vent, beaming up happily to another planet, or maybe an entirely new solar system.

And *that's* when I finally lost it.

Within seconds, a huge wave of self-pity seemed to crash over me, and I found myself laughing hysterically at the absurd depths into which I had fallen.

My God, what had happened?

Just one year earlier, I'd been the head of one of the largest state police agencies in the country! Before that I'd been the highly-regarded police commissioner who had done so much to make Baltimore safer!

Now here I was in the "Hole," clad in a sad clown costume of mismatched prison garb, lying on a dirty cellblock floor with my feet pressing a makeshift rat barrier against the steel bars while my cellies partied on, oblivious to my growing panic.

I stopped laughing soon enough; lurching right up to the brink of madness tends to be sobering after a few minutes. But all night long, the same thought looped over and over in my head:

How the fuck did they ever get away with this?

It was the lowest point of my life, by far. All I could see was darkness and despair, and my future going down the drain.

In the morning, we were marched down to the Atlanta Satellite Prison Camp, re-processed again for what seemed like the 100th time, and given another drab uniform of green pants and shirts.

Compared to leafy and open Eglin, the Atlanta camp was a bleak, forlorn-looking place. While it was still technically considered dormitory housing, we'd be living in a huge concrete enclosure divided into little cubicles with two beds each, giving it all the cozy ambience of a public bathhouse.

They stuck me in a cubicle with a guy named Eddie, a lean, muscular, dark-skinned Floridian who was serving a heavy sentence for drug dealing. When the older guys heard who my new roomie was, they shook their heads and laughed. Because Eddie, it turned out, was a genuine, 100 percent character.

For one thing, Eddie wasn't his real name, although that's what everyone called him. Secondly, he was always high. (Shocked that drugs are so widely available in a federal lock-up? Don't be. It's a fact of life.) He wore sunglasses day or night and talked nonsense to himself and never slept. Finally, Eddie had this singular trait: he wore three baseball caps – simultaneously! – each with the brim set at a different angle, the whole teetering mess perched on a doo-rag.

As it happened, Eddie was also the "Radar" O'Reilly of the camp. Just like the little hyper-active character on the old M*A*S*H TV series who seemed to be everywhere at once, Eddie could get you whatever you wanted, from God knows where.

The first time I met him, he asked if I wanted new Timberlands to replace the worn boots I was wearing.

"No," I said, "I'm good."

"OK then," he said with a shrug, and let the matter drop.

But the more you were around Eddie, the more you were convinced he could smuggle in anything from a case of vintage wine to a John Deere tractor – all for a price, of course.

He was my roomie for my whole stint in Atlanta. And we got along just fine after I laid down one important ground rule.

"Look, you can take whatever you want from my stuff," I told hm. "Just don't steal it. If you need it, just take it. And *tell* me you took it."

As they had at Eglin, random acts of kindness occasionally broke out in Atlanta. This was always amazing to me. You were in prison, you felt like shit, your whole life was fucked up. And yet there was this sense that you needed to help the other guy, both to reinforce your own humanity and because he might return the favor someday.

Case in point: when I first got there, I hadn't shaved in weeks, due to the fact there had been no commissary at Yazoo City to buy toiletries. I had a long beard and my hair had grown out, to the point where I was looking more and more like either Charlie Manson or the Unabomber, take your pick.

One day this Cuban kid came up and asked if I wanted a haircut.

"Sure," I said. "I'd love one. But I can't pay you right now."

"Don't worry about it," he said. And with that, he sat me down and shaved my head clean before trimming my beard with a set of clippers. It wasn't until weeks later that I could pay him back with fried chicken smuggled out of the kitchen.

(Yes, I was again working there with Dan Levitan. Dan's rep as a terrific chef was well-known by the Atlanta prison officials, and they were delighted when he offered his services. It was like a baseball team suddenly hearing that the top free agent on the market wanted to play for them.)

Life went on, but overall it was an edgier existence than at Eglin or Yazoo City. There were some seriously bad people in this camp, as we were to discover.

One inmate had his face slashed during an argument over a TV show. Not long after that, a prisoner standing next to me during a controlled movement began muttering darkly about how much he hated the camp and how much he wanted to go back up the hill to the Big House.

"I can't take this place anymore," he kept mumbling. "I'm going to knock somebody out . . ."

Sure enough, the moment they released us to walk, he clocked another inmate – laid him out cold. For this he was promptly taken away and locked up, presumably in the same cramped, squalid piece of steel-bar real estate he seemed to miss so much.

No, you definitely didn't want to screw around with anyone in this place. Stories abounded about inmates beating each other with soap bars or combination locks stuffed into socks, or heating baby oil in a microwave to throw in an enemy's face.

The inmate who disregarded – or failed to learn – the unspoken rules of the Atlanta prison camp could find himself in a whole lot of hurt.

One day not long after I arrived, for instance, I found myself showering next to this black prisoner. He was very squared-away guy – he might have been ex-military – and always had his beard neatly trimmed, his prison uniform neatly pressed and his shoes shined.

He was also a guy who never cracked a smile, never interacted with anyone and appeared ready and eager to kill someone over the slightest provocation.

Anyway, there were no shower stalls in the camp, only a common area with shower heads installed side by side and plastic curtains you could pull across for privacy. When we were both through showering that day, the black guy discreetly took me aside.

"Look," he said, "I know you don't know what's going on in here yet. But you *never* shower next to anyone."

Huh?

No one, he went on to explain, wanted someone's dirty shower water splashing on them. Therefore you always left a space between you and the other guy in the showers.

It was a valuable lesson learned, and maybe it spared me from getting my ass kicked – or worse – somewhere down the line.

Annoying behavior that would simply be ignored or laughed off in the outside world could also get you hurt in Atlanta.

An old Southern con man named Jimmy was a prime example of that. Jimmy was a rumpled sad sack with a perpetually runny nose who was oblivious to social cues, including the possibility that his behavior was pissing people off.

He would do stupid shit like walk all over the floors after the older cons had just waxed them, which would just drive them crazy. But Jimmy's most maddening trait was this: he would never, ever shut up.

Ever.

Once, just before Christmas that year, we were in a controlled movement to go somewhere and Jimmy happened to be next to me.

It was an awfully sad time for me. I missed my wife and kid terribly and the thought of spending the holidays without them was killing me. Now, standing in this sweaty, surly, heaving mass of prisoners, I just wanted to quietly wallow in my misery.

I wanted to be left alone.

But Jimmy wouldn't let me. No, Jimmy wouldn't stop talking.

I asked him nicely to be quiet. He kept jabbering. I asked him again in my most patient and respectful tone. Same thing: he just kept blabbing.

Finally, on the verge of losing it, I barked: "If you don't shut the fuck up, I'm going to go punch the guard and get myself thrown in the Hole, just to get away from you!"

An older black inmate – I'd later learn he was from Harlem – overheard what I said and laughed.

"You must be from New York!" he said. "Only New Yorkers talk like that."

But later, the same inmate would say of Jimmy: "That mother-fucker's gonna get hurt. We tolerate a lot of his shit 'cause he's crazy and we know he's old. But he better watch himself."

No, in prison, you couldn't always walk away from someone who was irritating the crap out of you, which led to an ever-present under-current of tension.

Despite the crowded conditions, intense loneliness was another condition most of us wrestled with in Atlanta.

No one had been able to visit me when we were locked up in Yazoo City, of course. Now, only the visits from my wife, my father and some of my old friends from the NYPD and Baltimore, helped alleviate the gloom.

The visits with Kate, though, could also be singularly humiliating experiences. The first time she came to see me, she was told her skirt was too short, which was against prison regulations. This meant she had to go to a mall to buy a pair of jeans before the let her in.

There was nothing private or intimate about these visits, either. There were guards all around the room, for one thing. You could touch your wife or girlfriend, but the guards watched carefully for any sexual contact. No one was grabbing any pussy or getting a handjob under the table, that's for sure.

Maybe what was most demeaning was that you were still counted during these visits. When it was time for the 10 a.m. count, for instance, you had to stand, line up and be counted off – all while your wife or girlfriend took in the whole dreary ritual.

Fortunately, only twice in Atlanta was my identity as a former cop nearly compromised – and both times I lucked out.

Once, I was walking by the TV room and saw, to my horror, my face suddenly appear on the screen.

What the hell?

It turned out the TV was tuned to ESPN, which was showing a re-run of the Leopard Games, the police Olympics where officers compete in running, shooting, traversing an obstacle course and other events.

Baltimore had hosted the games the year before and now ESPN was running an old clip of me being interviewed in full Maryland State Police uniform, including my Stetson hat.

Seeing this, I froze and mouthed a silent prayer: *Please don't let anyone recognize me! Please don't let my name flash up on that screen!*

Thankfully, the clip ended quickly and no one in the TV room said anything. It helped that my Stetson was pulled low over my eyes in the interview. What helped even more was that I'd been clean-shaven in that clip, whereas I looked like a biker gang leader now with a shaved head and ZZ Top beard.

The other time I almost got burned was while a guard was escorting me and another inmate to another part of the prison.

Somehow, the conversation between the guard and this other con turned to the types of surveillance tools used by law enforcement officials.

I was barely listening, until out of the blue, the guard turned to me and said: "Hey, *you* know. *You* were a cop. Tell him about the surveillance stuff . . ."

Even though my insides were churning, I managed to keep my voice calm.

"I don't know what you're talking about," I said, shooting the guard a dagger look that said: *You dumb motherfucker! Never do that to me again!*

In early December, while I was eating lunch in the dining room, one of the kitchen workers approached carrying a newspaper.

He stabbed a beefy finger at a small article on the front page and said: "Hey, isn't this the guy who did you?"

And there it was: Maryland U.S. Attorney Thomas M. DiBiagio, the man who had railroaded my conviction and ruined my life, was resigning from office under heavy criticism. Months earlier, the *Baltimore Sun* had published damaging emails that DiBiagio had written to his staff, urging them to make "front-page" indictments in political corruption cases.

The U.S. Justice Department had publicly reprimanded DiBiagio, and the *Sun* reported that in an internal review, prosecutors under the U.S. Attorney had said their boss should be removed from office. Well, he was gone now.

The news didn't totally shock me – I had been aware that Justice seemed unhappy with the over-zealousness of their top Maryland prosecutor. It gave me a measure of satisfaction, too. Maybe now people would see how dangerous a ruthless prosecutor out to grab headlines and further his career could be.

The news of his downfall also gave me a tiny glimmer of hope that someday I could be vindicated, even after my career had been de-railed and my life shattered.

Finally, in January of 2005, after what seemed like a lifetime, the day of my release was at hand.

Prison tradition dictates that all your buddies cook you a nice meal on the day before you get out. So some 10 of the guys with whom I played cards and bocce and smoked cigars chipped in a few bucks and bought food from the commissary, and this old Italian guy named Alfredo whipped up a pretty decent pasta meal with fish.

Naturally, though, the federal government found one last way to torture me.

In the middle of the meal, I was told to go see the camp administrator. When I got to his office, he leaned back in his chair and stared at me.

"The news media is here," he said. "And the word has gotten around that they're here for you."

Unbeknownst to me, reporters Richard Sher from WJZ-TV and Jayne Miller from WBAL-TV had flown down from Baltimore to interview me upon my release.

"So we're going to put you up in disciplinary segregation for your own protection," the administrator continued, "in case anyone finds out you're a cop and tries to attack you."

I couldn't believe my ears! They were putting me back in the Hole?! On my last night in this godforsaken place? So that I couldn't even say good-bye to anyone? Really?

"Look," I said, "I've been here for months and pretty much gotten along with everyone. I've had no problems in here. Don't do this to me."

But his mind was made up. I could see by his expression that pleading my case any further was just a waste of breath.

"No," he said, "the guards will come and get you soon and take you up the hill."

When I got back to the dorm, some of my buddies were looking at me strangely. Beyond the fence, they could see the street where a couple of satellite trucks were parked and TV cameras were already set up.

Finally this old Cuban motorcycle gangster, a dead ringer for Fred Flintstone with a thick body and head, turned to me and said: "Dude, who the fuck *are* you?"

My buddies who had been with me at Eglin knew who I was, of course. But the others in the room were stunned when I revealed my identity. Then, after a moment or two, everyone cracked up.

"No! We've been hanging out with the head of the Maryland State Police?!" someone cried.

"Yes," I said, laughing along with them. "Yes, you have."

As promised, a couple of guards appeared not long after to take me up the hill to the disciplinary segregation until. But when I groused about going, they looked at each other and shrugged.

"Oh, you don't want to go?" one said. "All right, I'm a big fan of 'The Wire.' Don't worry about it. You can stay here."

It was another act of kindness from another unexpected quarter in this hard place, another simple gesture of humanity for which I'll be eternally grateful.

Around 9 the next morning, right after breakfast, they processed me out. As I was leaving, a light-skinned black guy dressed in a suit and tie and looking like a buttoned-down professional, was turning himself in.

He was scared shitless, shaking all over and on the verge of tears. A guard kept trying to calm him.

"Dude, don't worry about it," the guard said. "It's not as bad as you think."

"He's right," I said, overhearing the conversation.

"But I didn't *do* anything!" the guy wailed.

The guard shook his head wearily and sighed.

"It's just a game," he said softly. "They do this to people all the time. Just come in and do your time."

To me, it yet another sad commentary on the whole system – this time from someone on the inside. And it reinforced what I'd thought all along: that so many of these incarcerations were not only unjust, but done for the most ridiculous of reasons, destroying families and ruining lives in the process.

Yes, that poor bastard would have to suck it up and do his time. But my time at three different federal prisons, thank God, was over.

My buddies walked me to the main gate. I gave my watch to one of them and my toilet kit to Dan, with instructions to give it to a new inmate who might need it. We said our good-byes with hurried hugs and a tinge of sadness; some of those guys, I knew, would remain there for many more years..

Through the fence, I could see Kate out in the parking lot, smiling and waving and looking drop-dead gorgeous, as always. Then I walked out and gave her a big hug and a kiss. It was January 19, 2005, a sunny and cold morning in Atlanta, and I was a free man for the first time in six months.

Jayne Miller and Richard Sher and their camera crews were across the street to greet me, too.

"When Ed came out," Jayne would later tell a reporter, "I thought: he lost weight! He was smaller! Here was the guy who was the police commissioner for two or three years and, yeah, it was kind of a stark difference to see him kind of stripped of all that authority.

"Prison's humbling. And he was definitely humbled. But he still had that confidence about him when he came out. He still had that swagger."

From there, we all drove to a nearby motel, where Jayne and Richard had rented a room so they could each interview me separately.

We kept the interviews short. They peppered me with questions about what life was like in prison and how did it feel to be out.

It felt *weird* to be out – that was the dominant feeling. But I was incredibly happy and excited, too. Yet all my emotions were still raw, and I broke down when one of them asked: "Do you still think you got screwed?"

"They shouldn't be able to this to people!" I said, the tears flowing freely now. "They just *shouldn't*."

From there, Kate and I drove to a hotel downtown. My father and my good friend Rick Burnham had flown down from New York to celebrate with us, and the two had already checked in. When Kate and I got to our room, she informed me we were all going to lunch at a fancy restaurant in Atlanta's posh Buckhead section.

"Uh, that might have to wait," I said, pushing Kate gently onto the bed.

(Hey, am I smooth or what? Fine, *you* try being the model of restraint after six months in the slammer.)

The meal that afternoon at the award-winning Restaurant Eugene was wonderful: steak, a few Manhattans and a lot of laughs. But nagging at me in the back of my mind was one of the questions Jayne and Richard had asked, namely: "What will you do now?"

The truth was, I had no idea.

I was 44 years old, with not a clue about what lay ahead.

And this terrified me more than anything else.

21
Stranger in an Even Stranger Land

Getting out was a bitch. The first few days were really hard – and *really* weird. It sounds counter-intuitive, but life seemed much tougher on the outside.

Think about it: when you're behind the fence, as they say, so is everybody else. So many of the other cons were angry men locked up for a long time, with far worse problems than I had. But there was a kind of commonality to our lives, too.

When you're locked up, you're all wearing the same drab clothes and eating the same shitty food. You're all not having sex, you all haven't seen your families and you're all living this miserable life.

But you're all living it *together.*

When you get out, now you're viewed as a pariah. You might as well walk around with a big scarlet letter on your forehead. "E" for ex-con, maybe. Because that's how people perceive you.

Maybe it sounds overly-dramatic, but it's not: your life is forever changed after a stretch behind bars. In the days and weeks after my release, that point was driven home to me constantly.

When Kate and I drove back to Tampa, I walked into a house I had never seen before and was greeted with a quizzical stare from a cute little five-year-old boy. I gave Jack a long hug, but the reconnection felt awkward.

He hadn't seen me in six months. Did he even recognize me? I wasn't completely sure. In prison, I would get him on the phone occasionally to say hi. But like most five-year-olds, he mainly wanted to watch cartoons rather than have a long, boring talk with his dad.

Now Dad was back home. And Jack was giving me these skeptical side-long glances that said: *So . . . you gonna be sticking around for a while this time?*

Here's another thing: you don't recognize how institutionalized you've become when you first get out of prison. And I had only been in for a very short time. I can't imagine how people who have been incarcerated for 15 years feel when they get out.

For some of those guys, when they're released, the world must feel like a completely different place. Now people are walking around with cell phones and iPads and watches that monitor sleep patterns and cardiovascular efficiency. Cars look different, fashion is different . . . it must feel like a parallel universe.

Even for a short-timer like me, the transition back to normal life was jolting. For days after I got out, I continued to walk around the house with my ski cap pulled low and headphones on, just the way I had behind the fence.

The weirdness of my new life really hit home when Kate asked me to help her cook dinner one night.

Understand, I'm not one of those guys who likes to do this. You know those guys you see on the TV commercials, the ones who are always smiling and sipping wine and having a great time cooking steamed vegetables or mixing a world-class salad with their wives?

I'm *not* that guy. Not even close.

But I agreed to help her, mainly because I was trying to be as nice and accommodating as possible after all the shit I'd put her through.

"How about peeling some onions?" she asked.

Onions? Sure. I could do that.

So I started peeling. And I kept peeling and peeling. And I didn't *stop* peeling until I had peeled the entire bag of onions.

When she finally looked up and noticed what I'd done, she gasped.

"What the hell are you *doing?*" she cried.

What?! I didn't know what she was talking about. I looked down at the empty bag for a moment. Then it hit me: I'd peeled enough onions to feed the Tampa Bay Buccaneers.

"I'm sorry!" I said. "It's just . . . I'm used to peeling 50 pounds of onions at a time! That's all I did inside!"

We both cracked up at the absurdity of the whole thing. Sitting in the next room, Jack had to be wondering what his mom and the weird dad with the ski cap and headphones were cackling about.

There weren't too many laughs a few days later, though, when a federal probation officer showed up to fit me with an ankle monitor. This was the official beginning of my six months of house arrest.

After a thorough search of my home for any weapons, ammunition and drugs, the officer clamped the ankle bracelet on me. It looked like a big dive watch and was synced to a box that would sound an alarm if I strayed too far from the house.

I was permitted to leave for only three reasons: to go to church, look for a job and work out at a gym. Now imagine what it was like trying to hide the ankle bracelet in a hot, humid part of the country like Tampa, where everyone wears shorts. (I ended up covering it with a plastic ankle brace.)

Trust me, all of these things take a terrible toll on your dignity and self-respect.

Here I had held a number of powerful law enforcement jobs and been an esteemed member of the community for many years. Now I was subjected to any number of horrible rules and indignities as an ex-con.

My probation officer turned out to be a total pro and was never demeaning in any way. But the cop in me noticed that when he visited my house, he always made it a point to park in my driveway in a way that blocked in my car.

Probation officers do this to ensure that no one tries to make a quick getaway during their visit, which often happens. If, for instance, an ex-con is doing drugs or has drugs in the house when the officer pulls up, he's likely to freak out and try to bolt so he's not violated.

But it really hurt to see the officer do this blocking maneuver on me.

Wow, I thought, *this is how I'm viewed now. This is who I am. I'm just another unpredictable bad guy who might cause trouble.*

If all of that wasn't degrading enough, looking for a job as a convicted felon multiplied the humiliation factor by a thousand.

Seeking employment, by the way, isn't something that's simply *suggested* by your friendly neighborhood federal probation agency. No, you're *mandated* to do it upon your release from prison. You must go out every day and document your search for work. And once a month you are required to document how much money you made, how much you have in your checking and savings account, and whether you have acquired any storage space – including a post office box and safe deposit box – that could be used to hide anything.

So here I was, the former boy wonder of the NYPD, the former police commissioner of Baltimore, the former superintendent of the Maryland State Police, applying for all these menial jobs, most of which were meant for kids.

I hit every fast-food place you could imagine: McDonald's, Chick-fil-A, Krispy Kreme, etc. I applied at Harley-Davidson, hoping my knowledge and passion for motorcycles might be an in. I loved to work out, so I applied to every gym in Tampa. And I loved nice clothes, so I hit every men's store in the city, too.

On most of the applications, one question stood out as if flashing in neon on the page: have you ever been convicted of a felony? Of course there was only one way for me to answer.

Filling out the ubiquitous "Employment History" section was even more depressing. How was that going to look? *Yes, even though I was once one of America's top cops, I am now eager to sell jelly doughnuts and watery coffee to surly office workers at your fine establishment! No, really I am!*

Finally, after looking and looking for work, I stumbled into Caswell-Massey at Tampa's upscale International Plaza and Bay Street mall. Caswell-Massey was a high-end perfumery. The company had been in business for hundreds of years; one of its colognes was said to have been a favorite of President George Washington.

That was pretty cool to know. But this was even better: the application didn't ask about prior convictions. So I filled it out.

And somehow I got hired!

The woman who ran the store was really sweet to me, too. I ended up selling men's and women's products and did so well that eventually I was given the keys to the place and allowed to open in the mornings.

As dispiriting as the rest of my life was, I actually enjoyed the job. It felt good to be useful again. And being able to leave the house every day was a godsend.

Yet less than six weeks later, I got a call at home one day from the store manager. The tone of her voice was funereal.

"I don't even know how to say this," she began. "But I have bad news."

Right away, I knew what was coming.

Sure enough, she said someone had called Caswell-Massey's corporate headquarters and told them who I was, and about my past life. Corporate had called the store manager right away and told her to fire me, on the grounds that I had lied about my background on my application.

This was completely untrue. While I had never been asked about a prior conviction, I had noted that I was a retired police officer. But that didn't matter now. The decision had been made. I was history at Caswell-Massey.

"I'm really sorry," the store manager told me. "I know you didn't lie."

"OK," I said, "should I bring my keys in?"

"You don't have to," she said. "They already made me change the locks."

As the realization of what had happened sunk in – *I just got fired from a minimum wage job! At the mall!* – I was devastated.

You wonder why so many ex-cons go back to their criminal behavior? The answer's simple. They have to make money somehow! Now here I was, jobless, broke and required to go back to Baltimore in a few weeks to start my community service.

Which was when the bad luck that had dogged me for so long finally began to turn.

Within days of my perfumery career coming to an abrupt halt, I got a call from Andy Graham, my lawyer. He had just heard from Bob Phillips of CBS Radio in Baltimore.

Phillips had told him that a local station, WQSR, had just polled its listeners, asking this question: "Now that you know the prosecutor in his case was fired for essentially targeting high-profile cases, would you want Ed Norris back as police commissioner?"

The response was over-whelming: some 90 percent of the respondents said yes. Apparently, I was still wildly popular with a large swath of Baltimoreans. Who knew? Now Phillips wanted to know if I'd be interested in doing some sort of call-in talk show with radio station WHFS, providing the details could be worked out.

So what did I do?

Did I leap at this incredibly fortuitous lifeline being thrown to a down-and-out ex-con who'd just been fired from the mall and was drowning in debt?

Did I shout: "HELL, YEAH, ANDY! ASK 'EM WHERE DO I SIGN?"

No, I didn't. At least not right away.

See, I was still white-hot angry at the world. I especially hated everyone and everything that had to do with Baltimore. In fact, I felt so betrayed by the city that I had even gotten rid of all my Ravens and Orioles gear. (Just *looking* at them practically brought on PTSD.)

So, no, the last thing I wanted to do was talk about my train-wreck of a life and how it went off the rails – especially on a stupid radio show with producers and on-air talent I didn't even know. Or trust.

No thanks, I told Andy. Not interested.

Except . . . then I *was* interested.

After a few hours of soul-searching, I realized I was being stupid. *Heck,* I thought, *I'm not doing anything else. No one wants to hire me down here. And God knows I need the money.*

So I called Andy back. He must have thought I was nuts.

"OK," I said, "tell them I'm interested."

The whole thing seemed ludicrous on the face of it. Someone would actually *pay* me to be on the radio? And people would tune in to listen to what I had to say?

What a concept!

The truth was, I didn't know what kind of fresh hell I was getting myself into.

But I knew this: it couldn't be worse than the hell I was already in.

22

Phoenix Rising

The ground rules for my radio segment were simple: I'd call in at noon each day to talk about my dumpster fire of a life and also offer thoughtful and provocative opinions (he said modestly) on the news of the day in Baltimore and everywhere else.

At least that was the plan.

The station had its affiliate engineers in Tampa come to my house and install an ISDN line, which improves the quality of phone conversations. And the next thing I knew, I was a regular on "Out to Lunch" with co-hosts Chad Dukes and Oscar "The Big O" Santana, doing the show from my little office in the back of my 1,050-square-foot house while my crazy Giant Schnauzer, Max, barked wildly in the background.

Even though most of the callers seemed supportive of having me on the air, part of the shtick was for me to engage with the ones bent on tearing me a new one.

Some of them were vicious bastards, too.

Over and over again, the haters would call in to rant that I was a thief, a crook and a despicable human being who should never be allowed to work again.

It was exhausting to keep interacting with these people. But somehow I did. What else did I have going on? We talked about politics, crime, music, sports, my story, Baltimore stuff – the show had no grid whatsoever.

My job was to chime in and be outrageous, which was easy enough. Plus they were paying me $500 a month. Which meant I was employed – I was still doing "The Wire," too – so it kept the feds off my back.

Yet at the same time, something else had me totally freaked out and paranoid for weeks: my ankle bracelet kept going off, even when I was sitting in the house. Which meant I was getting calls at all hours of the night and day from the probation service charged with monitoring that I was home.

"Yes, I'm right here!" I'd say each time they called. "I don't know why this is happening! I haven't moved!"

Naturally, the probation people – who don't exactly deal with choir boys on a regular basis – were suspicious.

"Well, did you go outside?" they would demand. "Did you go to the store?"

"NO!" I'd shout over and over again. "I HAVEN'T LEFT THE HOUSE!"

The more it happened, the more nuts I became, cursing and raging that the government was doing this on purpose just to fuck with me. I was driving Kate crazy with my paranoia, too. Finally we found out, to my immense relief, that it was the radio equipment that was somehow triggering the bracelet alarm. A technical adjustment quickly fixed the problem.

Somehow, my little segment on "Out to Lunch" became so popular I was offered a one-year contract to do a three-hour daily show called – ta-daa! – "The Ed Norris Show." So when my home detention sentence was up and I returned to Baltimore in August to begin doing my community service, I was also launching a new radio show, with producer Maynard Evans soon assuming a bigger on-air role after the firing of the Big O.

That first day back in the city after being away for so long felt totally surreal.

When Bob Phillips and a couple of other station executives took me to a nice steakhouse in the Inner Harbor and we walked around after dinner, people came up and hugged me. Cops on the street smiled and saluted me. I didn't know what kind of reaction to expect, but I sure didn't expect to be greeted like that.

Two days later, I nervously reported for the first time to my new probation officer, Chris Keating. No, "nervously" is putting it too mildly. I was practically jumping out of my skin, pacing back and forth in the waiting room like a leopard in a zoo.

In Tampa, I had felt safe; here in Baltimore, there were enemies all around me. My case had been so contrived and trumped-up, all I could think was: *What will they try to do to me next?*

I was still wildly-paranoid about violating my probation, both from the ankle bracelet mysteriously going off and from getting fired from the perfumery. In Baltimore, if I was living in a house with, say, even one old shotgun shell lying around, they could violate me for possessing *that,* never mind owning a firearm.

Or they could violate me for talking to a stranger in a bar who turned out to have done 10 years in the federal pen in Lewisburg, which meant I was consorting with a disreputable person, a big no-no.

But as soon as I met with Chris, the knot in my gut loosened.

"Relax," he said with a smile. "You were treated very badly. That ends today."

The new radio show went well from the get-go, too. I lined up a bunch of big-shot guests like Gov. Ehrlich and my old NYPD boss Howard Safir, for the debut, and after that we were rolling.

It was classic shock-jock radio. We'd have strippers and porn stars on, including the legendary Ron Jeremy, the world-record-holder for most appearances in adult films, if you follow that sort of thing. But we'd also talk sports, entertainment, politics, the economy, policing in Baltimore – whatever the listeners wanted to chew over.

Trying to do the required 500 hours of community service, on the other hand, was extremely difficult. I worked at first for Catholic Charities, doing maintenance work at a house they ran for drug-addicted kids.

But I was only working there a few hours a day, so I supplemented that by walking dogs for the SPCA. Still, I wasn't getting enough hours doing that, either. How long can you walk dogs every day? I didn't want to find out.

Finally, someone suggested I check with the League for People With Disabilities – and that's when I found my niche.

The League worked with both the permanently disabled and with those recovering from traumatic accidents. My job was to check people in and help them with their rehabilitation, show them how to lift weights safely and work the exercise machines. It was like being a trainer in a gym and I took to it immediately.

All the while, though, it was a lonely and trying time. My family was still living in Tampa and I was flying home every weekend after the Friday show and flying back Sunday night.

The station had been very good to me, doubling my salary before my one-year contract expired, putting me up in an apartment in the suburbs and getting me endorsements (Air Tran, Victory motorcycles) that suited my lifestyle. But the commute back and forth to Florida was killing me, as was not seeing my wife and son nearly enough.

Once I completed my community service, I went to station management and said: "Look, I don't have to be in Baltimore anymore. I'd like to stay, and if you give me a real contract, I'll move my family up here. But I can't handle the travel."

Management was again unfailingly generous, giving me a new two-year deal with an option for a third year. Unfortunately, I had far less luck pursuing something else that would have made my life easier.

In addition to six months of imprisonment, my original sentence had mandated three years of probation. But Chris Keating had told me from the beginning that he thought I was a perfect candidate for early termination of probation.

"Clearly, you're not a criminal," he'd said, which I greatly appreciated.

But when he submitted my name for early termination to the U.S. Attorney's office, it was denied. They said I wasn't a good candidate, which made me absolutely furious.

Let's see, a former big-city police commissioner and state police superintendent who got fucked over with this trumped-up, bullshit mortgage charge – *I'm* not a good candidate?

Who's a good candidate then?

Colin Powell? Mother Theresa?

I still had a lot of anger in me, and hearing about stupid decisions like that from ruthless, vindictive bureaucrats who controlled my life didn't exactly make me more placid. Unfortunately, the anger could come out in ugly ways, too.

One night, I was having dinner and drinks downtown with Maynard and Chad and some others from the station when this young guy in his 20's began hassling me.

He and his friends were standing a few feet away from us at the bar, and he kept looking over at me and muttering "They should have never let that guy out" and "They should have put him away for 10 years."

He'd been drinking, of course, and his voice grew louder and louder. He knew I could hear him, too – that was part of the game plan.

Finally, I had enough.

"If you want to say something to me," I told him, "just fucking say it."

Puffing up his chest, the guy got right in my face and continued his rant. He pushed me and I snapped immediately.

Seconds later, he was on the ground and my friends and I were quickly making our exit.

End of story?

Uh, no, not exactly. That would have been too easy.

Instead, on the show the next day, Chad Dukes suddenly began regaling the listeners with a spirited account of Eddie Norris' run-in with the drunken blowhard.

"Yeah, Eddie knocked this guy out last night after the dude got in his face!" Chad began. Frantically, I gave him the "kill" signal while shooting him with an icy glare that screamed: *Dude, what the fuck are you doing?!*

Sure enough, that night, as I had dinner with an old friend in a suburban restaurant, I got a call from my friendly neighborhood probation officer.

"I heard something on the radio today," Chris Keating began.
Uh-oh.

"I heard about what happened in the bar with that guy," Chris went on. "You know, you can't get involved in assaultive behavior."

I stammered out a lame explanation about my co-host totally exaggerating the incident, spinning a fantastical story for the listening audience just to kill time.

"It was all bullshit, Chris," I said. "Just radio shtick. You know how it is. There was nothing to it."

But when I hung up, I was soaked in sweat. My stomach was doing back-flips. Chris seemed to believe me, but I was already beating myself up

Holy God, I thought, *how stupid can you be? Getting into a bar-fight? In your situation? After all they've done to you?*

Yet after that first year out of prison, as the months passed and my radio career progressed, as my family and friends stuck with me and the good people of Baltimore continued to embrace me, I was feeling better about life.

I was not the Eddie Norris of old – those days were gone forever. And this new version of me was darker, more cynical, less trusting. But somewhere inside, I could feel my soul again. Slowly yet steadily, I began to sense that maybe things would be OK after all.

Not that I ever wanted to erase the memory of what I'd been through. In fact, late in the summer of 2006, I decided I needed a permanent reminder of that awful period of my life, and all that I'd survived.

So I had a big tattoo of a phoenix rising done in the middle of my back. I wanted it to hurt, too. I wanted to feel the pain and the soft trickle of blood that would seep out with every jab of the artist's needle.

Because I never wanted to forget what they put me through.

EPILOGUE

Much has happened – some of it bad, a lot good – in the 12 years since the dark days of my conviction and incarceration. From that terrible night in the Hole in Atlanta, I have almost returned to being someone I recognize in the mirror.

In 2009, I starred in the Discovery Channel documentary "Jack the Ripper in America." The premise was that when the world's most notorious serial killer was finished with all his nasty business in London, he started a fresh killing spree in the U.S.

Partly because of my work on "The Wire," but mostly because of my real-life experience investigating homicides and creating the NYPD Cold Case Squad, I was cast as a detective looking into the plausibility of such a scenario. I flew to London and got to do some cool things, like reading the original case folder and drinking in the same Whitechapel bar where Jack picked up his prostitute victims.

The Discovery people liked the show so much they approached me about working on other unsolved mysteries, such as whether Hitler really did kill himself. But a change of regime at the channel resulted in all those projects getting canned, and that was the end of my documentary career.

Sadly, and yet inevitably, my wife and I grew apart in the years after my imprisonment.

My divorce from Kathryn was finalized in the spring of 2010. It wasn't just the womanizing that caused it. I became impossible to live with after what I'd been through. Anger and depression dogged me. At times, I was so low I couldn't get off the couch.

Anxiety and paranoia were also constant companions. If the government could railroad me that easily, inventing bogus charges fueled by an ambitious and ruthless prosecutor, what was to prevent the feds from circling around and taking another whack at me?

During the divorce proceedings, I was seeing a therapist for all my issues.

One day I sat there and poured out my whole sad story. I ticked off all the things the sham felony conviction had cost me: money, employment, reputation (the dreaded Google hit), family, social life, hobbies.

I'd lost my right to bear arms. All my law enforcement buddies had to stay away from me, because they couldn't be spotted talking to a known felon.

When I was through, the therapist was silent for a moment. Then he shook his head softly.

"I've never seen anyone lose so much in one incident," he said finally.

Ohh-kay, I thought. *Well, that's not really helping me, doc.*

Here was a person who saw broken people every day. And basically he was telling me: "Wow, you got screwed over worse than anyone I've ever seen."

In any event, Kate put up with it all – the surly prolonged silences on my part, the wild emotional swings, the furious eruptions and hours and hours of venting – until she couldn't any more. I will grieve over that loss for the rest of my life. Thankfully, though, we get along better now than we have for years.

As for my son, Jack, Kate and I shared joint custody, but his age and my work hours necessitated that he live with his mother. Jack is a senior in high school now, an A student and a track star who will go on to college in the fall. He's a wonderful kid and I bought a house near Kate's, in a small town in Carroll County, Maryland, so I could stay close to him.

My father died in November of 2016, just a few days before Thanksgiving. He was 82. A New York Police Department honor guard presided at his funeral and I was given the departmental flag that draped his coffin.

It was an incredibly emotional ceremony. Just as with line of duty deaths, my dad's funeral warranted a bagpiper playing a stirring version of "Amazing Grace." As I do every time I hear it, I wept. I've heard that song played way too many times over the course of my lifetime, for too many brave police officers taken far too soon.

As for my mother, she suffers from Alzheimer's and doesn't know my father is gone. Nor does she know who I am. I miss them both.

What else can I tell you about my new life?

I still work in radio all these years later. These days I'm the co-host, along with Rob Long, of "The Norris and Long Show" on Baltimore's leading sports-talk station, 105.7 The Fan.

It's not a bad gig at all. I make more money than I did as police commissioner. My bosses treat me well, and I'm not exactly breaking rocks in the hot sun. I have a nice car. And the people of Baltimore treat me incredibly well.

Case in point: after breakfast in a South Baltimore diner recently, I reached for the check, only to see it snatched from my hand by a man who was eating at the next table with his daughter.

"I'm buying for him," the man announced to the owner. "Because of all he did for the city."

"Uh-uh," the owner replied with a smile. "We already picked it up."

People are always telling me "You're doing great! You gotta be content, right?"

But the answer is no.

I didn't do anything wrong. I'm not a crook. Yet I have to live with the stain of that pejorative forever. (Or until I get a presidential pardon, something I'm actively pursuing, even though the odds are long.)

Worst of all, I can't be a cop anymore. I can no longer work in the profession that I loved, the profession in which I excelled, the profession in which I was respected and admired.

I tell people all the time: "Being a cop is what I was *meant* to do. And I was really good at it. If your mother was the victim of a crime, you'd want me to have the case."

All these years later, I still replay all the events that landed me in a federal prison at what should have been the prime of my life. I'm still convinced it was a political hatchet job. But whether it was spurred in part by my post-911 criticism of the FBI or a mayor envious of my popularity and enraged by my defection to the state police, I'll probably never know.

Most likely, I was simply the victim of an ambitious and unethical prosecutor attempting to further his career by destroying mine.

But what I want people to understand is this: although I've recovered in many ways – at least in a relative sense – 99 percent of the people the government does this to are crushed and never recover.

Shit happens in life, sure, but the feds have no business destroying marriages and families. I want people to understand the viciousness of this process. Essentially, the government used sex to blackmail me into a guilty plea, with the mortgage letter as their trump card.

I want people to compare whose sin was greater, mine or the government's. And I want people to know how common this really is.

Still, there's no question that the entire ordeal has changed me profoundly.

I used to be passionate. I laughed a lot. I loved hard and hated even harder. There was not much gray in my world. Now I laugh less. I don't get sad, but unfortunately I'm never happy, either.

It's been a dozen years. I thought I'd be over it by now.

Now I'm pretty sure this is who I'll be for the rest of my life.

FINAL THOUGHTS

It will come as no surprise to learn that I pay close attention to cases where the miscarriage of justice is glaring. Cases such as the one that shattered the Duke men's lacrosse team, where innocent kids were nearly railroaded into prison by an unscrupulous prosecutor, Mike Nifong, for a rape he knew had never been committed. Cases such as the ones involving the six Baltimore police officers whose lives were offered as a sacrifice to an angry mob following the death of Freddie Gray and the rioting that devastated the city. That is the real reason that I wrote this book.

I wrote it because the American system of justice has been abused by so many for so long it is now broken. But like the mythical frog in the pot of water that's heated a degree at a time so the poor dumb creature doesn't jump out and is instead complacently boiled, our system's decline has taken place over so long that we've just accepted it.

"Justice for all" and all that happy horseshit about the U.S. being the gold standard from criminal justice in the world is simply not true. Sure, it makes for great speeches on the Fourth of July. But in my opinion, we have one of the most corrupt and dangerous systems of justice in the world.

Too often, innocent people are targeted to launch the careers of unethical prosecutors. Yes, as in most professions, the vast majority of prosecutors are good, ethical people who entered their field for pretty much the same reason I became a police officer. The problem is a belief that America can arrest its way out of its problems, which allows evil prosecutors to masquerade as dedicated crusaders for the public good until they're finally exposed, as mine was, and as Mike Nifong was.

Think about the following facts and come to your own conclusions: The U.S. has more people incarcerated than any country on earth. According to the Bureau of Justice Statistics, in 2013, this country had the largest prison population in the world, with 2,220,300 people incarcerated. The U.S. was second in per capita prison population, but only because the nation ahead of us was the tiny Seychelles, which had 735 people incarcerated in a country of 92,000.

More appropriate comparisons are to other developed countries. While the U.S. had an incarceration rate of 698 per 100,000 in 2013, other developed nations weren't even close. Canada had 106 per 100,000. Greece had 120. Spain had 141. Japan had 49. If you compare the U.S. against itself historically, the reason for the high rate becomes clear: imprisoning people has become big business in our country, led by a misguided war on drugs.

Today there are over two million drug offenders in federal and state prisons, as well as in county jails, in the U.S. When the country celebrated its bicentennial, there were 262,833. If the fact that 10 times more people are imprisoned in America now compared to 40 years ago isn't shocking enough, consider what Adam Gopnik wrote in a *New Yorker* article in 2012 titled "The Caging of America": "Over all, there are now more people under 'correctional supervision' in America – more than six million – than were in the Gulag Archipelago under Stalin at its height."

If you couple the rate at which we imprison people with the fact that a defendant has essentially zero chance at a fair trial once indicted, especially in the federal system, then you might understand why I and many other people who believe they were innocent opted to plead guilty to crimes they believe they didn't commit.

Oh, yes, another pertinent fact: nearly 100 percent of people indicted by the federal government are convicted. And be mindful that a grand jury indictment requires the same burden of proof as when a police officer arrests someone on the street: probable cause. That's certainly a low bar, is it not? So if you believe 97-99 percent of people accused by the federal government are guilty, you're living in a fool's paradise.

Just pray your tax returns are in order and you never do anything to piss off someone in a position of power.

The way it really works is this: someone (a prosecutor) decides you're a big enough target to propel his or her career forward and you're investigated. This is important because, while under state laws the police investigate crimes and endeavor to solve them by finding the guilty party, federal prosecutors often find targets (their term, not mine) and then "build" cases using whatever "crimes" they can find or come up with.

In other words, they decide someone is a bad actor and load up enough charges so that the risk of proving one's innocence at trial simply isn't worth it.

In my case, my attorneys were told by the feds that if I didn't take a plea to the bullshit charges they had drawn up, I would never see my son grow up. Faced with the prospect of losing at trial – of the 1-3 percent of people who actually go to trial in federal court, only about 8 percent are found not guilty – I would have pled guilty to killing JFK to be able to raise my son.

It's not supposed to be this way, or at least that's what I naively believed all my life. I thought justice was possible in America. I now no longer do.

Now the lines from the Bob Dylan protest song "Hurricane" keep rattling around in my head. Dylan played fast and loose with the facts of Rubin "Hurricane" Carter's sensational 1966 murder case. But he got this part right:

> *How can the life of such a man*
> *Be in the palm of some fool's hand?*
> *To see him obviously framed*
> *Couldn't help but make me feel ashamed to live in a land*
> *Where justice is a game.*

About the Authors

ED NORRIS is the former police commissioner of Baltimore and former superintendant of the Maryland State Police. Before that, he had a prestigious 20-year-career with the New York Police Department, beginning as a patrolman and rising to the rank of deputy commissioner of operations at the age of 36.

Norris had a recurring role on the HBO hit police drama "The Wire," appearing in 22 episodes over five years, and was the star of the 2009 Discovery Channel documentary, "Jack the Ripper in America."

He is the co-host of the popular "Norris & Long Show" on Baltimore's sports-talk station 105.7 The Fan.

He lives in Carroll County.

KEVIN COWHERD is the New York Times best-selling author of "Hothead" and five other baseball novels for young readers written with Hall of Famer Cal Ripken, Jr. This is his fourth book of non-fiction for Apprentice House Press.

Cowherd was an award-winning sports and features writer for the *Baltimore Sun* for 32 years and has written for *Men's Health, Parenting* and *Baseball Digest* magazines. A collection of his newspaper columns, "Last Call at the 7-Eleven," can still be found in fine remainder bins everywhere.

He lives in northern Baltimore County with his wife, Nancy.

Apprentice House is the country's only campus-based, student-staffed book publishing company. Directed by professors and industry professionals, it is a nonprofit activity of the Communication Department at Loyola University Maryland.

Using state-of-the-art technology and an experiential learning model of education, Apprentice House publishes books in untraditional ways. This dual responsibility as publishers and educators creates an unprecedented collaborative environment among faculty and students, while teaching tomorrow's editors, designers, and marketers.

Outside of class, progress on book projects is carried forth by the AH Book Publishing Club, a co-curricular campus organization supported by Loyola University Maryland's Office of Student Activities.

Eclectic and provocative, Apprentice House titles intend to entertain as well as spark dialogue on a variety of topics. Financial contributions to sustain the press's work are welcomed. Contributions are tax deductible to the fullest extent allowed by the IRS.

To learn more about Apprentice House books or to obtain submission guidelines, please visit www.apprenticehouse.com.

Apprentice House
Communication Department
Loyola University Maryland
4501 N. Charles Street
Baltimore, MD 21210
Ph: 410-617-5265 • Fax: 410-617-2198
info@apprenticehouse.com • www.apprenticehouse.com

CPSIA information can be obtained
at www.ICGtesting.com
Printed in the USA
BVOW11*2057050417

480308BV00001B/1/P